THE MEANINGS
OF LOVE

THE MEANINGS OF LOVE

ALAN STORKEY

INTER-VARSITY PRESS

INTER-VARSITY PRESS
38 De Montfort Street, Leicester LE1 7GP, England

First published 1994

British Library Cataloguing in Publication Data
A catalogue record for this book is available from the
British Library.

ISBN 0-85110-988-8

Set in Linotron Baskerville

Photoset in Great Britain by Parker Typesetting Service, Leicester

Printed in Great Britain by Cox & Wyman Ltd, Reading

*Inter-Varsity Press is the book-publishing division of the Universities and
Colleges Christian Fellowship (formerly the Inter-Varsity Fellowship), a
student movement linking Christian Unions in universities and colleges
throughout the United Kingdom and the Republic of Ireland, and a
member movement of the International Fellowship of Evangelical
Students. For information about local and national activities write to
UCCF, 38 De Montfort Street, Leicester LE1 7GP.*

Contents

Introduction

GETTING LOVE WRONG

The failure of love?

The study of love presents us with a powerful dilemma. On
the one hand, it is a word which has millions of supporters.
Each generation gathers round it like fans at a cup final.
They not only chant the word in public but also profess it
in private on a lonely walk, in bed, in a letter or just to their
own hearts. On the other hand, there are millions of well-
intentioned people who have seen the word turn to dust in
their lives. Every night men and women sob as they realize
that for them love has died, and the next morning the ache
of the loss is etched into their faces. For some, the experience starts early as they recognize that their parents do not
love each other and probably do not love them either.
From this start, they can go on a quest to find love again, or
even accept that probably the world is a loveless place.

Every day our culture is saying these two things. First,
love is basic to our human experience, and we must have it;
but, second, we must doubt whether it can ever work. The
cynics are getting younger, and some of them are turning
their backs on love before they reach adolescence. How do
we understand this contradiction, and where do we stand
in relation to it? Do we believe in love, or mistrust it? But
there is another question which comes before this
dilemma. *What is love?* It is this question which is the subject
of this book.

If love is good, we cannot ignore the sheer scale on which
we get it wrong. The magnitude of the problem is partly
conveyed by the rates of separation and divorce throughout the world, which often run at a quarter or a third of all
marriages. Even within marriages and relationships which

7

last, love often turns out to be defective or destructive, and none of us knows the extent of private suffering which occurs under its label. Most of us can recall times when what we believed in good faith to be love turned out harmful or destructive to our partner in some way. We set out on the journey of love, but never get there. What starts as love can easily change into recrimination, longing, tension and distant relationships. Thus, most of us have some experience of being failed lovers or of being let down by others, and the people who are blandly free of this experience often cannot see the hurt they are causing. This is a pattern common enough to deserve some thought and analysis.

Consider a typical situation. You know Henry and Anna quite well. You value their friendship. They are both pleasant people and have a lot to give, and they are in love. Yet, as their relationship develops, it turns sour. They come to view each other negatively; and each sees the other person as the problem. But the Henry and Anna you know have not changed. Whatever has been going on, there has been no dramatic change in either of them to explain the falling in and out of love. The issue must lie with the role love played in their relationship. It needs investigating.

Or consider an explanation which is commonly given for the breakdown of relationships. 'We were incompatible. That time round, I did not meet the right person, and I had better try again until I do.' Despite its frequency, this remark does not square with the evidence we obtain from the larger picture. Most of us know of marriages in which the partners are strikingly different from each other, and yet they get on well together. Some couples live quite contentedly with almost all kinds of 'incompatibility'. Yet statistics suggest that the people who try again tend to fail again. It also seems odd that in certain countries and in certain eras a high proportion of the population seems to get the choice right, while at other times and in other places it goes wrong. Thus the idea of incompatibility as an explanation is a gloss added after the event; it does not fully address what is happening in these millions of cases of the breakdown of love. We are looking at a cultural pattern which occurs across eras, classes, countries and continents. The modern cultural movement towards high levels of divorce has even crossed the old barrier between communism and capitalism, for the marriage patterns of Russia and Eastern Europe have looked very similar to those of the United States or Canada. This suggests that something bigger than mere personal incompatibility is going on. Indeed, this 'something' seems to trap people, so that they tend almost automatically to get love wrong.

Models of love

Our way into the issue is to look at the meanings of love. What people mean by love differs. Sometimes, when a husband tells a wife how much he loves her, she thinks or says, 'But it's not that kind of love I want.' What we mean by love has consequences for relationships, and some of the meanings and the consequences are not good. This study looks at a few key meanings and where they lead us. If we mean different things by the love we offer one another, then at the very least there is likely to be misunderstanding. Some of those kinds of love will probably be mistaken and will snarl up relationships. If many of the meanings of love which are accepted by most of us are misguided, then, in so far as we are shaped and influenced by them, we walk into messed-up lives. It is therefore worth analysing these meanings and what consequences they have when we follow them, so that our love is not blind.

This book will set out the models of love which we often espouse, show where they lead, and explore their inner logic. We shall investigate each of the meanings of love in its own terms, with examples of the kinds of relationships it generates. There is no suggestion that any one person or relationship can be described by a single model, but that each model significantly influences our culture. Each model is therefore set out as a group of attitudes, ideas and motives which have obviously and publicly influenced the way we think about love. In order to present each model, we shall examine its characteristics and follow through the kind of response it evokes. The aim of this analysis is to involve its readers directly, for we all need to scrutinize our own relationships in the light of each 'meaning' of love. The book's underlying purpose, then, is not just to examine what is the case in our culture but also to offer readers some categories by which they may examine what is going on in their own lives. It is a very personal task, for we may not know what even our friends mean by 'love'. Analysing it is an intimate business. This book outlines a number of different attitudes to love which we can recognize and identify as having some influence on our lives. Although these attitudes do not occur in pure forms, they have an inner logic and coherence which demand commitment and lead to certain consequences. Seeing them as discrete types helps to analyse the effects they have on us, and possibly to see the resulting tensions in ourselves and in our relationships.

This book offers a critique of a number of views of love which are common in our culture, and then goes on to point to something better. If a man is totally obsessed by a woman and wants to possess her completely, so that he hunts her and plots to make her his own, something is wrong with the meaning of love which grips his life. It leads him astray and causes tense relationships. But at the same time he loses out on a better meaning of love – love in its tenderness and openness. Where is this love to be found? It seems to be a rather well-guarded secret!

The conviction underlying this study is that it lies with God. We are going to argue that the true meaning of love, full-blooded, sexual, passionate and Christian, is found in the relationship that each of us has with God. If this is the case, it fits current circumstances, because the Christian meaning of love does not receive much publicity among the media voices we shall be examining. While this study is not an exhaustive investigation of the Christian meaning of love, it will point to some of the Christian characteristics which have been ignored and sublimated in our culture. Readers who are not Christians will therefore find that we touch on the issue of conversion. They should not be surprised. Most of us, when we get love by the tail, do not succeed in taming it, but get pulled in new directions by it. So if we take on love and God at the same time the end of the journey might well not be where we expect.

But this is true not just for those who see themselves on the outside of Christianity. Christians, who might believe that they knew something about love, can be locked into narrow and self-congratulatory models which do not really work. Love is the great leveller. It is no closer to any of us than we are to God and to each other. The Christian faith does not own love. Jesus was quite clear about the difference between the woman who washed his feet with her kisses and dried them with her hair, and the Pharisees. She loved, and their neat formulations were full of dead men's bones. All of us are therefore on dangerous ground. What we prize highly as love might be dismissed by God and what is undervalued might turn out to be dazzling beauty to those who see afresh.

What this book is not

Quite rightly, some readers will already be wondering at the vagueness of our use of the word 'love'. It seems to mean boy–girl stuff, but surely Christians are more interested in the love of God and of our neighbour. This books does focus primarily on man–woman relationships – romance, sleeping together, cohabitation, sex, friendship, affairs and marriage. It is actually even more limited than that, since there are many important dimensions to man–woman love which this study does not explore. It is worth mentioning some of them so that the limitations of what follows are clearly evident.

First, the development of our personal ways of loving, and our ability to love, grow out of our family and social background; this deeply shapes each of us, but is not studied here. Secondly, the personal and sexual identities of men and women are important for the way they love, but these are not the focus. Thirdly, there are cultural patterns of love in, for example, the United States, India, France and Uganda, which are not explored. Fourthly, there is each person's spiritual walk of love or pride or hatred which, also, is not directly touched. Again, patterns of personal damage, healing, failure and lostness, which are a part of many people's love history, and which need to be opened up in different ways, are passed over here. This study also ignores love of family, neighbour, enemy and country – large and important parts of people's lives. Most importantly, there is the question of the truth of our relationship with God, which shapes the quality of what we often call 'love'.

All kinds of aspects of each person's development and identity, then, are important for the kind of love they can offer and receive. They are scarcely addressed here. All these limitations reduce the scope of this study of man–woman love. (It thus fits in, for a while, with the idiom of narrowing the meaning of love to sexual relationships.) Yet because the destructive power of mistaking the meaning of love is so great, man–woman love is a large enough theme for any number of books, and certainly for this one.

It is worth noting at the start that this study does not focus on love as a moral question, concerned with right and wrong conduct. Those who take this approach seem to have no problem either in understanding life or in deciding what good love is. The problem of identifying and living in true love, however, is much more complicated; our motives, understanding, personalities and sense of what is good are so messed up that important questions occur long before people get to what is right or wrong. The truth about love is in itself an open and important question. Indeed, the idea of 'morality', tied as it is to the notion of carrying out a principle formed in the mind, is actually a very limited view of the way people operate. It is not a biblical idea, but one which stems from eighteenth-century thought in assuming that the rational individual relates to other people through morality. By contrast, this study is unashamedly sociological; it recognizes our dependence on the views, attitudes and culture of others, and the way we relate to God communally. So this study, while, we hope, not 'immoral', is quite strongly anti-'moral'.

To sum up, our central argument is that the biblical reality of love, rooted in the very character of God, has been obscured by counterfeits which form the predominant understanding of sexual love today, and it is these which cause our problems. The evidence for the argument lies in the inner contradiction which each of the meanings of love examined in the following chapters contains. They promise hope and fulfilment; but, when their implications are fully unrolled, they offer kinds of love which fail us. If this is substantially true, our study should help us to see, without cynicism, the gentle power of true love in our lives.

Chapter 1

IDEALIZED LOVE

One common perception of love is of something we strive towards – an ideal. It is what we work and long for. To be in love is a state which we hope will not just be over the rainbow, but will arrive; the rainbow will end in the garden and stay there. Some enchanted evening you will see your true love across a crowded room, and the chemistry will happen. Of course, we are too sophisticated to be taken in by out-of-focus pictures and gush, but the ideal is there as a reference point to which we continually return. It may start out as naive and become more sophisticated, but it underlies our reactions to others and shapes our emotional development. Love is an ideal, and if it is not there, we want it to be, longing for it to happen, or mourning because it has gone.

The pattern is one which occurs in many different forms. There is the ache in the heart of the teenager, vaguely focused on the poster every morning and evening. In our early twenties we may have a quite definite image of the girl or man who will make life fun and who has got what it takes. Middle-aged people begin to feel a slight panic that they have not met the right person; or, if they are married, might begin to imagine an alternative to their real-life spouse – the wife who understands and never nags; the husband who tidies up, talks vivaciously and is never absent-minded. (Perhaps the alternative model in the wife's mind spends more time with her than does her husband, so that when he is present he experiences a vague sense of disgruntlement that he is not like the model.) Sometimes love itself is idealized; at other times the person is the ideal. Let us look at these in turn.

Ideal love

Ideal love is a blissful state where nothing ever goes wrong or causes disagreement and tension. It involves two people coming together and being at one with each other, enjoying fun, relaxation, empathy and a good time. It is the one relationship where the problems that occur in other relationships are not repeated, so that it remains unspoiled and good. It contrasts with the indifference and dullness of daily life. Many locations convey just such an experience – the honeymoon suite, the intimate restaurant with the candle-lit meal, the tropical island holiday – because people will pay almost anything to get it, even for a short while. People long for deep understanding, for the look which betokens ultimate togetherness, for the sexual encounter where the earth moves, or just for a sense that things are right. If we feel that the ideal is present, we are in a state of euphoria; if absent, we enter a period of yearning or anxiety. Or we feel deep nostalgia, hoping for the time when it will return. The power of the ideal is so great because what is sought is so good. We may moderate our hopes, but usually the vision of intimacy, love, care, beauty and communion knows no gainsaying.

The ideal often takes very different shapes. He thinks love is never having to say that you are sorry, and she that clearing the air is the best way forward. He thinks love is coming home, and she that it is going out. His vision of the honeymoon and hers do not match. Usually, of course, the ideals are not polar opposites; they are subtly built up from experiences with parents, peers, dating and work. They are continually refined in our minds and hearts, fed by daily-life constructions, daydreams and media fictions which happen to appeal to us. 'Jim knew that this was the love he had been looking for. They swam, lounged in the sun and played games. Even shopping was fun. It was easy to love and care for a girl like this, so different from the catty remarks of June and the others at the office. For a moment his brow creased, but then Doreen leaned over and put some more suncream on his face.' (We, of course, are more sophisticated than that.)

The force of these ideals can be felt by focusing on a quite common one: the ideal home, which is important to many couples. If the locus of the marriage is perfect – the perfect bedroom, the kitchen where every meal is a partner-pleasing creation – then, of course, the marriage will be perfect too, and love will reign. Many rich people live their messy lives in near-perfect homes, looking for the cleaner which will finally cleanse away the personal problems which still seem to hang about. Redesigning the kitchen becomes a substitute for sorting out a relationship. The quest, as they move from one home to another, is for the ideal place, for the reappearance of the magic. Of course, people move house, install new kitchens and lay new carpets for other reasons. But the advertisers know how deep are the yearnings and hopes to which they are appealing. Sadly, the displacement of effort to the new home or decor often detracts from the relationship which is the source of the yearning.

Ideal love, then, is thoroughly our creation, and often sets the terms on which others are to relate to us. It contains our own weaknesses and embodies them in our definition of love. It may be a problem to others who have to cope with our ideal of love and conform to its demands. Or perhaps it seems to them like a crinoline; it swirls round us, keeping others at a distance. They must either tread on it, to our annoyance, or blow kisses across the gap, while we live oscillating between the ideal and the daily reality.

The ideal partner

The quest for the ideal mate is a similarly powerful motive. Who is the person who will meet the hopes and desires of my heart? Again, the picture is often strongly shaped by friends and the surrounding culture, carefully thought out and quite specific. The wife must be domestic, or a bombshell; she should put her family first, or she should play golf. Dating agencies and friendship advertisements list the kinds of characteristics desired. One 'Heartsearch and Romance' column produced requests for attractive, slim, lively, unstuffy, good-humoured, intelligent, caring, feminine, non-smoking, fun-loving oriental women with high standards. The man still has to be tall, dark and handsome, with intelligence, warmth and a sense of humour. Sometimes the shopping-list of characteristics is so long that it narrows down the candidates to three of the world's population.

Usually, of course, the ideal is much more open; it may be vaguely shaped by media stars and other personalities. For most of us, it receives much of its shape from our parents – even without articulating it, we might aim to marry somebody who is like, or a modification of, Mum or Dad. At this stage we notice how strong an agenda this ideal can create; it involves expectations and requirements of the other person which, even if they are unspoken, can powerfully influence the terms on which the relationship proceeds. The verdict that 'he is not my type' often registers the extent to which the actual misses the ideal. It also conveys how dismissive this idiom can be, as it casually sidelines thousands of people on the basis of what has been generated in our heads.

Sometimes we see the ideal mate as having strong sexual attributes. At its simplest level this is expressed in macho images of men and sexy images of women, but actually the matter is far more sophisticated. In the West, sexual images are a major growth industry. They are idealized according to different stereotypes in film, magazine and book, and are often developed through daydreaming and fantasy, which engage quite a lot of people for two or three hours a day. The images play on certain traits, which change. The dominant, strong, decisive male may give way to the sensitive, gentle, caring one, or the soft, responsive woman to the interesting woman with initiative. But the power of the ideal remains to shape its devotees, firming up the requirements which they will bring to their daily relationships. Pornography is an extreme form of this kind of idealized sex which feeds the fantasies of those who are searching for it. Sometimes women in the West feel required to look 'sexy' in ways which would call into question the ability of couples in the poor world to make love. This requirement in turn can become linked to the idea that a partner should perform sexually in a certain kind of way, so that, instead of being in bed on their own, a couple have thousands of other performing couples with them in their heads – an appalling thought.

There is a flip side to this search for the ideal mate. Many people feel pressured as they try to live up to the ideals created by those they know or hope to know. Early on in relationships, this often takes the form of an awareness that the 'real me' is not what my partner thinks I am like, and, if he discovers the real me, then he will lose interest. Millions of women have laboured, in their psyche or in their relationships, under the burden of being compared with some cult female or with the star attraction at the office. Their lives revolve around the wish, 'If only I were like her.' There is the ridiculous advice, purveyed by several North American books and magazines, that a wife should wake up early and 'put on her face' before her husband wakes up, so that he will find her looking nice. It is this idiom which makes underarm hair 'disfiguring'.

Many women's concern with their shape, dress, weight and appearance partly grows out of a strongly internalized ideal. Anorexia nervosa, compulsive clothes-buying and obsessional plastic surgery all give evidence of the power of these ideals to control people's lives. Pregnancy becomes a major crisis for many women and men who live their lives in this idiom; the full, rounded tummy is a threat to the ideal figure on which they believe the relationship is based. One of the greatest successes of the women's movement is its fight against the tyranny of this attitude, if need be by wearing overalls and smoking pipes. The freedom from this pressure is well worth the battle, but the problem still lies with those who nurture and impose the ideals. Many women and men struggle for years to find and to be what their partner's ideal requires, until the impossible task becomes obviously so. Others fight for the emergence of the 'real me' from under the ideal.

Once upon a time, a young man fell in love with a girl. She was beautiful and gentle and had green eyes. He wooed her, and the time came to ask her to marry him. He saved up and bought an emerald ring to match her eyes. They went with subdued awe to their favourite spot, hired a boat and rowed out to the middle of the shimmering lake surrounded by rustling trees. He took out the ring, looked into her eyes, and thought carefully. Then he threw the ring over his shoulder, and asked her to marry him. At first she was a bit taken aback, but then she accepted – comforted by the knowledge that the ring at the bottom of the lake meant he loved this *brown*-eyed girl (who had forgotten her contact lenses) as much as he had the green-eyed one.

The pressures are also applied to men by women. Until recently, female expectations of their partners' dress, physique and appearance have been more muted, and the ideals have been present in more psychological terms. One of the most powerful ideals grows out of the situation of the woman at home, often with a family and domestic pressures, whose husband works long hours into the evenings and weekends. To compensate, she uses romantic novels, magazines, soaps and videos to create an absorbing ideal who is different from the man she actually lives with; he relates to her and is attentive to her needs. Sometimes, this romantic ideal is vested in an attentive male who happens on the scene, but more normally it stays as a kind of hidden rebuke which never gets addressed or properly discussed. The man is vaguely aware that he should be someone else, but it is not clear who. At other times, the pressure is imagined and not real; the husband believes he should be strong and masterful, when she prefers sensitivity and some help around the home.

Many of us feed into this already complex picture ideals of ourselves and of our own love. We feel, for example, that there was never love like ours. We are patient, caring, thoughtful and prepared to put up with a great deal in the name of the love we have for our partner. Occasionally, we feel the need to point out how marvellous our love is, because it is not being fully recognized; and we may be shocked to find that what we have seen as so fine is actually valued less highly. It turns out that our sacrifices work out to our own benefit. We do the garden or mend the car to escape from more demanding commitments. The chocolates we buy are the ones *we* like, and the great gesture of love and devotion is an act which we are prepared to bask in for the next ten years. Not only is our love idealized, but so is our personality. We are never unfair, always patient to the limits of endurance (a useful contradiction in terms), and really quite witty, good-looking, and not a bad catch. These illusions may be challenged, but they often flourish through all kinds of bad weather.

Analysing the ideal person

We are now in a position to see how complicated are relationships based on idealized views of love. It is possible for there to be eight different 'personae' taking part in a single relationship. The woman may consist of herself, her ideal self, the man's ideal of her, and her view of the man's ideal; while the man is sometimes himself, his ideal self, her ideal of him, or his own response to her ideal. Even if not all of these personae are working at the same time, the relationship between them can become highly complex. Sometimes the real persons are too worn out by the complexity to put in an appearance!

Crucial in this situation is the point at which the weight of commitment lies for each of the partners. If a wife will not let go of a certain ideal of herself, although the husband loves and enjoys her as she is, then there is a tussle which needs resolution. If the wife is confronted with the ideal woman (in terms of appearance, sexuality or education) which she knows she is not, then the tension between his ideal and who she really is can dominate her life. Sometimes, in resignation, one partner decides to leave the ideal undisturbed rather than face the upheaval which disclosure would bring. The overall effect is to leave the participants with feelings of unreality, not knowing where they are, always searching for the other person, and even of not knowing *who* they are. This poses a serious danger, destructive to the relationship and to the persons involved. What started out as an ecstatic hope of love seems to work out as damaging and harmful.

Bob felt he could handle money well; his brother had taught him quite a bit of accounting, and he had looked after the football club accounts for two years. But actually he was not very good at planning expenditure. Jeanette came from a family which had repeated problems with debt and was glad that Bob was so much in control financially. Her illusions were shattered, however, when they went into the red after their first holiday and had to pay a surcharge. From then on she took over the accounts. It was difficult, and the whole process filled her with foreboding. Meanwhile, Bob had recognized his tendency towards extravagance, and cut back. As a consequence their finances were continually healthy. Yet Jeanette put this down to her own handling of the accounts, and unnecessarily continued to do them. The cost, however, was a continued sense of anger at the way Bob had let her down. Because Jeanette was living with her shattered ideal, she could not see how competent he was.

The problems are deep as well as complicated. Inseparably linked to the ideal is disillusion. Indeed, the meaning of 'wedding' contains this for many people. The wedding and honeymoon leave a memory which she can remember for the rest of her life when the dull routine takes over. The older couples look on and say, 'It's nice while it lasts.' At a recent wedding I was struck by the intensity of the custom of sabotaging the honeymoon car, and, if possible, the honeymoon. Why do 'friends' laboriously sew up clothes, arrange for raw meat to be placed in the bridal bed, and get the honeymoon car labelled as a stolen vehicle? Perhaps it has something to do with the cynicism of the disillusioned, which makes it difficult for them to look again upon the bliss for which they hoped. The ideal and the reality must face each other, and when this happens it is often accompanied by blame, cynicism, disrespect, and even hatred. The dynamics vary.

'If you were such-and-such a person, we wouldn't quarrel.'

'If that's what you're really like, I don't want to know you.'

'If that's what you think of me, I'll leave.'

Behind all these confrontations lies the gulf between the ideals and the real; the struggle of people to be what they are not; the searches that are rooted in fantasy, and the driving power of the self-defining ideal. Because this kind of blame is a deep denial of who the partner really is, its destructive power is very great.

Other forms are less intense. Many couples who reflect on their conception of love will find that it fits a pattern of repeated striving and failure. Often the early anguish of the failure will lead the couple in the end to settle for something less; the ideal floats above reality not as something to strive after, but as a warm, nostalgic memory. There is the ideal, which is love, and the reality, which is something slightly different. Life is tinged with a continual experience of the second best.

The source of the ideal

Where does this approach come from? Although it might seem very contemporary, it actually has a long and supposedly noble heritage. To understand it properly, we would have to trace it back to Greek ways of thinking which have had a profound effect throughout Europe. One can see evidence of this in museums or art galleries. The beautifully proportioned male and female statues (even if some of them have lost an arm) show us this classical Greek ideal. It is there, too, in the idea of the perfect athlete, the ideal behind the Olympic Games. So it should come as no surprise to discover that the ideal is basic to Plato and other Greek philosophy.

But of course it did not end with the Greeks. The same attitude spread throughout Europe and deeply influenced the Catholic Church. 'Platonic love' was a high-minded celibate relationship which was often defined by the church as the best kind of love. In the medieval legends, the search for the Holy Grail was intertwined with the search for ideal love; it was a long and arduous quest which would eventually result in the attainment of the ideal. Knighthood, with its valour and purity, displayed the kind of nobility which could reach this ideal. At the same time it was often seen as *un*attainable; it would corrupt. In the most famous English legend of all – the love of Arthur and Guinevere – the relationship which was to be the inspiration for the whole of England was corrupted by Launcelot and then by Mordred, striking with tragedy the whole court of Arthur. In Italy a different tradition developed in the late thirteenth century. The idealized woman was fused with the cult of the Virgin Mary, so that, since then, Mary, as virgin, pure, maternal and demure, has been the archetype for millions of women world-wide, and the ideal to which they must conform.

Although more recent thinking has lost many of these Greek overtones, the underlying conception remains. The ideals change with culture, but have remained powerful. In Jane Austen's time, the ideal woman was a person of sense and sensibility, who played the piano well, engaged in good works and graced the drawing-room. The social historian E. J. Dingwall describes how nineteenth-century genteel American wives were so put on a pedestal and literally out of touch that the husbands engaged in sexual activity with the slaves and servants.[1] Nineteenth-century women's fashions tell us a lot about the ideal woman of the period; the tiny waspie waist was achieved by corsets which meant that their wearers could scarcely walk across a room, let alone do domestic tasks. It was indeed a mark of high masculine status to have such an ornament as a wife.

This attitude highlights a development in idealism which continually recurs. In reaction to the ideal with its antiseptic feeling, many opt for the real; to know life, warts and all. The realist writers of the nineteenth century, such as Balzac and Dostoevsky, sought to lift the veneer of civilized ideals and to reveal the murky reality. Yet there is a sentimentality here too. To love the warts-and-all villain, embracing the smell, is no answer either, because we all have flaws which can be dangerously sentimentalized. Edith Piaf's 'Non, je ne regrette rien' was powerfully sung, but stupid. In more recent times this see-saw between ideal and reality is reflected in television advertisements. Heroic, unattainable love has enthralled us, but it is also a joke. Most of us, when we reflect on it, will be amazed at how power-fully the notion that love is unattainable has been conveyed to us. If we believe this view of things, it is not surprising that we go around with an air of tragedy, sad that what we most desire seems permanently beyond our grasp.

When we wake up to the problem, we also realize the motives which often generate these ideals. Many of them are a kind of escapism: 'If only life was like this,' or 'It's not really my fault,' or 'If only the other person would change.' It is from our own inadequacies that these ideals of love, ourselves and the other person are generated. They often reflect a pattern of scapegoating in that we run from true love and a true understanding of our weaknesses into creations which leave our mistakes unchallenged. Yet, of course, the idealizations merely make the failures deeper and more intractable. How good, then, to move away from these illusions!

Post-idealist love

The process of discarding the illusions involves us in call-ing into question our idealizing of love and our creation of ideal images of ourselves and our partners. The problem arises because our ideals bear the taints and distortions which we create in them, and because we seek to live in ideals in order to escape what might be true of ourselves and of others. Biblical understanding requires us to with-draw from these mistakes. Our identity is given by God, and our own understanding of ourselves and others is a fallible and very incomplete construction. Our identity is not something which is constructed by our own intellects. Indeed, the Bible is rather stern about this possibility. Just as we are to create no false images of God, so we are to create no false images of those whom God has made. To bear false witness of one another is to transgress one of the fundamental commandments of the creation. We are God's creation, and are not to arrogate to ourselves the business of defining what other persons should be like. For our ideals are always, so to speak, computer simulations, far less rich and wonderful than the real hands, hair and eyes of the loved one. This truth is reflected in the experience which many persons trapped in idealist relationships have. They know that they are very much more wonderful than their partner has realized, and they are right. The problem of the partner who has not found his (or her) ideal is really that he has not discovered the person with whom he is living. If he listened, looked and understood, he would see how much more wonderful is the created person. When we have been messing about with ideals of ourselves or others, to move back into the central truth of our created identity before God is like coming home. At a level deeper than any of us understand, we can take our shoes off and be ourselves.

There is also a critique of ideal love. The kind of love the Bible requires us to show to one another is patient and kind; it seeks the good of the other and does not bear grudges. It can be done now and with those we know. It is a command, because those are the absolute terms on which other people should be addressed. The commitment of marriage is more specific, but it rests on this same normative basis. There is no need for an ideal, because kindness and patience are always possible. The ideal is for those who are on the run, who are looking for special conditions, who want to be over the rainbow rather than getting wet. Love in Christian terms refuses to be an ideal, and remains a do-it-now requirement, because we are made to love, and to give ourselves to God and to one another. Where we fail, we have to face it and change, not set off on some illusory quest.

The glory of the gospel lies in the countless examples of Jesus meeting people who were sick, proud, quarrelsome, aggressive, failures, afraid and lost, and loving them. He did not idealize or flatter his disciples or the religious leaders, but treated them straight. It is the love that can look anything in the face and respond with care, hope and faith. All of us have some inkling of this love as the way to live; we live in God's creation as he has created us. Yet the broad and stable basis for life given by God's love for us is obscured by the idealizations which are peddled in our culture. We had all far better pull away the ideals and gaze at one another face to face to see the aweful beauty of who we are.

Chapter 2

THE FEELING OF LOVE

When we talk about falling in love, it often means succumbing to an emotional state. It involves a deep longing for the beloved, and includes a set of emotions – fear, elation, peace, joy and anxiety – which are heightened and which dominate daily events. There are few of us who are not gripped by some of these emotions at one stage or another, and many feel as if they are going down the tubes in a total experience. 'Falling in love again' is a process of self-abandonment which is as complete as being in free fall. There is no going back, and the experience has to be followed through to its conclusion. People who let love take over like this describe themselves as 'soft', 'gluttons for punishment', or 'incurable romantics'. Others react against this way of entering a relationship, and fight to stay in control of themselves. *They* will decide whether they fall in love or not, by a deliberate act of the will, not by fatalistically keeling over. They will keep their emotions firmly limited to certain areas of their lives, making sure, for example, that they do not get in the way of career and work. Even at first glance, therefore, we can see deep ambivalences in the role of emotions in love and in life. We usually experience longings, aches, hopes, empathy and concern for the other person which weave through our lives and colour the cloth. Our emotions also register the hurts of love as though they have been run over by a bulldozer. But what these feelings mean is far from clear.

What are emotions?

The nature of emotion is a mighty subject. But the emergence of 'emotions' as a distinct concept is itself interesting.

It is a word which really arrived only at the end of the eighteenth century, when states of feeling became thoroughly dissociated from ideas and cognitive processes. Since then, the distinction between thinking and feeling, reason and emotion, has become commonplace. People often argue that the one does not and perhaps should not involve the other, So it is especially important to think things through dispassionately before the feelings are engaged. Others note that since love is a matter of the heart and not of the head, falling in love is not a result of rational reflection. Freud held that a barrier separated the emotional, pleasure-seeking centre of our lives from the external controlling mechanisms of our minds. He saw adult love as continuous with, and rooted in, childhood sexual and pleasure-seeking feelings.[1] On this understanding, many of our thoughts are rationalizations that justify our deeper emotional commitments.

Let us discuss some of the issues which arise from these points.

First, and in contrast to the view just described, we have to accept that emotion does involve thought. Often, we think most deeply about ourselves emotionally. Our feelings bring together the commitments and directions of our lives. If their inner meaning is unclear or inaccessible to others, it is probably because we think they will not understand, or because we do not trust them, or because we find our feelings too complex to communicate. Most of us think about our feelings, and feel about our thoughts. Every thought we have, then, is played to some emotional tune which expresses how we stand in relation to that thought. (Often, but not always, speaking conveys that tune better than the written word.) Indeed, emotions are often a crystallization of reflection and judgment. Frustration, for example, is a common emotion which we feel when our minds are unable to work something out (whether a child with a puzzle or a physicist with a theory); it expresses a quite complex conclusion that no solution is possible.

A second common twentieth-century misconception is that emotions consist of basic drives (such as sex, survival or avoidance of pain) which are essentially primitive animal instincts.[2] Much of the work done by behaviourist psychologists was based on this assumption. A similar tradition locates feeling in the subconscious, out of which it comes to conscious life. Most contemporary work has moved beyond these gross assumptions, but the underlying error still needs to be addressed. It roots feelings in primitive responses which are 'really' about sex or comfort or pain; they are to be explored, understood and controlled. Such a view of human psychology is defective, however, because it fails to recognize our complex emotional development. Our feelings reflect our past, motives, faith and understanding of ourselves. Recognizing our own feelings and those of others can therefore be a complicated task. For example, many of us experience tensions in our emotional lives because of contradictions in our thinking and attitudes; these are often quite sophisticated problems. By contrast, crude responses such as uncontrollable rage, phobia and exaggerated elation may signal a breakdown in healthy emotional responses.

A third misconception is that everybody's feelings have the same roots. As we develop as individuals, however, so do our own unique emotional maps. Straightforward situations can produce wildly different emotional responses in different people. Imagine five people, each alone in a house. One of them misses others. One enjoys the solitude, while another fears the isolation. Someone else feels compelled to work hard. Another is just bored. These emotions take shape in the framework in which each person lives. This shaping of emotional development will be our special concern in this chapter, although it will also be important throughout the book. For our individuality means that being in love can take many different forms, some of them good and healthy, but others destructive. The real challenge for lovers is to distinguish carefully which is which.

Finally, emotions reflect our relationships. Being with someone is much more than a set of ideas; it involves commitment, care, patience and pleasure – responses which are not segregated from one another, but unified in their focus on the other person. These responses are two-way. We feel such-and-such about another person, and we feel that person's reaction to us.

Sometimes these feelings are mistaken; we did not properly know what we felt, or we misunderstood the response offered to us.

This suggests a deeper conclusion. Emotions can be true or false reflections of our lives. A manic-depressive person experiences emotions which are, superficially at least, not appropriate to the immediate situation. When someone's emotional responses do not seem to fit what we expect, we regard him or her as behaving oddly. But in a deeper sense we may all be behaving oddly, in that many of our emotional responses are not true to our own lives or to those with whom we live. Children often experience their parents' irritation over matters which have nothing to do with them. We may have feelings of love which are not matched by actions reflecting genuine love. Such 'love' is a kind of emotional hypocrisy; it floats like a sentimental cloud above the needs of the other person. Or a misdirected feeling of love can lead to insensitive and hurtful behaviour. Our feelings, therefore, must be subjected to careful scrutiny. They can be shaped for good or ill; they can reflect the truth or a lie. They can represent true or false love.

A short history of emotional types

These points suggest that emotions are not a separate domain of life, but closely integrated with all we think, value and do. There are strong trends in our culture, however, which invite us to adopt a stereotypical emotional map. We shall try to identify some of these, especially since they can get in the way of open emotional responses. We shall look for a number of historical types which have emerged from and since the Enlightenment.

The modern history of emotions begins with a male assertion of the centrality of mind, thinking, understanding and mental control in masculine life. 'I think, therefore I am [a man].' Men were to be educated, to think, to philosophize, to be men of affairs and of state, and to run life on the basis of their understanding. On this model, emotions in men either did not exist or were to be suppressed as irrational. The mind told the body what to do, and usually it obeyed. Emotions, like benevolence, pleasure-seeking and duty, were subject to rational moral control and ensured an ordered pattern of living.[3]

Women, by contrast, were feeling-centred; they could not think, and the meaning of their lives was found in men and relationships. They were expected to faint, cry, swoon and clasp their hands to their bosoms. Although the double standard was not new, this was the culture in which it developed more strongly. Women were supposed to be naturally faithful to one man, who would meet all their needs, emotional and sexual; while men's bodies were seen as much more likely to develop multiple sexual attractions which they would sometimes try to fulfil, but which were supposed not to affect their minds. Thus, within this idiom, male sexual urges were relatively detached from emotional commitment, while women were faithful and wanted to get their man. Their sexual relationships were more strongly associated with childbearing, housework and death in a way which gave them a different, more fearful, character. The two types emerging from this culture are therefore the supposedly rational, emotionless male, and the feeling-centred, irrational woman.

The second polarity concerns emotional domination. Men, because they had economic and physical power, were used to exerting emotional control over relationships. This often involved the suppressing or dampening of male emotional responsiveness (the 'stiff upper lip'), but it also required the women to support the emotional tone established by the men. When men scattered their emotions of anger, irritation, need, impatience and having fun, women were expected to come behind with a brush and pan and tidy up. This requirement would often be backed up by orders, threats or violence. The aggressive male was complemented by the blotting-paper wife. Women became used to absorbing and submitting to the terms expressed by the men, and to having their forms of emotional expression dictated by them. Only in relationships with children and with other women were they able to step outside this demure, imposed pattern, and many women had too little time free of work to open up these areas of emotional expression. Male control of language and formal education were ways of muting women.[4] The normal course was for the woman to spend her time reading the emotional state of her spouse and tending his moods in order to preserve equanimity and to be the great soother. The cost down the years has often been women who were severely depressed.[5]

A great change occurred in the nineteenth century, however, under the influence of the Romantic movement. This allowed middle-class men to have feelings, sentiment and soul; it opened up to them the possibility of experiencing the pangs of love and of wringing their hands when it was not requited. Male poets became national figures. The overriding message was one of romantic love. 'Come into the garden, Maud, because I want you to be the inspiration of my life.' So the Victorian man would drop to his knees and plead for the love of his maiden. His emotional attitude was akin to worship. He would go further, and say that his very life depended on it; and he would have read many contemporary authors, poets and artists who reflected similar attitudes. It is easy to be amused by this Victorian man, but it is worth noting two of his characteristics: first, the great emotional freedom compared with previous eras, and, second, the emotional faithfulness of this romantic attitude. Nevertheless, the pattern remained one in which the man expressed his worship in song, opera, poem, art, courtship and dress, while the woman became much more fully the recipient and inspirer of emotions. As heroine, sacred figure, mother, or even as Queen Victoria, she was the fount of male emotional life; but (except for the work of some female novelists) women's feelings could be given relatively little expression: she was statuesque.

Yet, at the same time, the Victorian era was one of great moral dominance. Men were expected to be upright and moral, but often failed to be so. Men's emotional energy was channelled towards correctness and a sense that they were living above criticism. This was accompanied by attitudes such as sternness, inflexibility, a dependence on rules, and a distrust of emotions (which might lead people astray, and which evidenced moral weakness). Within this framework, emotions were likely to be evil, and therefore had to be contained by firmness and moral control. Women were seen as partners in this enterprise, except that their moral goodness was shaped by submission. They would do what they were told because it was infallibly good. On this model, it was unnecessary and even wrong to feel; the main issue was proper behaviour. Thus we have the upright (even uptight) male and the pious wife.

This attitude, however, produced its own reaction. To be 'naughty' was to experience all the emotions which were immoral. These were by definition enjoyable, because they were devoid of the stern correctness of moralism. The music halls and other kinds of entertainment, including drunkenness, offered an emotional escape from the old straitjacket. What was perceived as moral was now seen as boring. The process of seeking enjoyment directed people's lives, producing either the hearty male or the jolly wench.

Another major change happened towards the end of the last century. Emotions became much more subjective. They were what people felt inside, and had no obvious connection with public life and external relationships. Being in love was part of a personal quest which had no internal relationship with marriage, faithfulness or even with the other person. Individuals had inner dialogues with their feelings, but there was not necessarily much sharing or communication. Emotion became a silent, subjective truth which was often intrinsically private. Being in love was an experience accompanied by elation, sorrow, daydreaming, sexual expression and intense relationships, but all of this was part of an individual or even an existentialist journey. Emotions were inexpressible. People's experience might meet for a while; they might touch flesh, but the feeling would not last. It was merely a stage in a longer journey in which everybody was alone. Feelings changed with the journey, and had no stable moorings.

Alongside this emotional attitude to love stands another which has been deeply formative in the West. It is the idea that the man expresses himself through his work, his physical strength and his presence. He must, above all, avoid any show of emotion which would compromise or undermine his male identity or communicate how he feels. There are many different types of this basic model – the strong, silent macho man who can take anything thrown at him; the unexpressive, often lonely and inarticulate, manual worker; the efficient professional man who is in control; the public-school adult, with his stiff upper lip, who was taken from home at the age of seven and put into an emotional cage. D. H. Lawrence fought this emotional poverty of both the public-school adult and the Nottinghamshire coal-miner. Deep into all these types is driven the idea that emotion and weakness are linked. To avoid expressing emotions, or to suppress them, requires certain difficult kinds of behaviour. A grunt, or a cup of tea, will express a year's devotion. Being in love is strictly taboo.

Women have to accommodate to the relationships set up on these terms in a number of ways. One is to reveal emotion, exposing their weakness in order to assure the male that his strength is needed. Another is to fight the male power by generating feelings which will prise the man out of his emotional armour. Many women end up living the emotional lives of two people as they constantly interpret what their husband is feeling but never says or shows.

These developments yield fourteen emotional types which we can list. Although they are too stereotypical to fit any individual absolutely, most of us have probably been influenced by one or more of them. Sometimes, of course, the gender of the type may be different from the one identified here.

1. *Mr Reasonable* – 'I think and then act; feelings get in the way.'
2. *Mrs Swoon* – 'My feelings often get the better of me.'

3. *The Boss* – 'I'm doing important things; make sure I am not upset.'
4. *The Soother* – 'My job is to keep my male happy.'
5. *The Romantic Man* – 'She is the inspiration of my life.'
6. *The Madonna* – 'I am the great mystery and he worships me.'
7. *Mr Upright* – 'I live a moral life and keep my emotions firmly under guard.'
8. *Queen Victoria* – 'We are not amused.'
9. *Edward, Prince of Wales* – 'Mum didn't have much fun and I'm going to make up for it.'
10. *Marlene Dietrich* – 'I'm naughty and I like it.'
11. *The Marlboro Man* – 'I'm lonely and nobody understands me, but I've got my horse.'
12. *The Mask* – 'Nobody knows what I feel like inside.'
13. *John Wayne* – 'I'm strong, but there's a soft core inside if you can get to it.'
14. *The Wife of Bath* – 'We know what the men are feeling, don't we?'

The point of listing these types is not to label individuals, but to describe some emotional idioms which have great power in our culture. Sometimes the types are just amusing: the woman who sighs at John Wayne is actually married to him. More often, the problems which arise from these typologies are sad; the 'Madonna' closes off her emotions as a way of giving herself power, creating distance where there should be intimacy. The Marlboro Man marries the Wife of Bath and feels even more alone when he has been 'explained'. These emotional journeys or pilgrimages involve basic mistakes. They lock their adherents into idioms which do not allow a full emotional response. They distort the potential of the whole person, born in God's love, to enjoy emotional freedom.

The emotional orchestra

A Christian perspective places our emotions in a rich context of response to God, to ourselves, to other people and to the rest of the creation. A true feeling of peace is a melody played on many instruments. Yet twentieth-century emotions have become increasingly narrowed down to the response of the human subject. As individualism has become rife, the focus of emotional inspiration is how the individual feels. We construct our world from the inside outwards, and no longer have a home in relationships with God, with the community and with the natural creation. On this view, being in love is primarily 'what I feel'. Love is whatever emotions arise for me as a result of a close relationship with a man or woman. Historically, of course, much of what is felt as love grew out of a Christian culture. Love was felt as kindness, care, patience, trust and tenderness, and it still is by millions because these characteristics are basic to the created *structure* of male–female relationships. They express the terms on which men and women are called to love one another. But another cultural development has been at work, expressing the outworking of humanism, in which people's emotions are a law unto themselves and take off in whatever direction is dictated by the heart. Here we must see a crucial difference between Christianity and humanism.

Christianity affirms the importance of emotions in people's lives. Even more decisively, it identifies them in Christ's life and in the responses of God to humankind throughout history. We should beware of anthropomorphizing God's attitudes towards humans, making them into the kinds of sentiment which we happen to feel, for we would then run the risk of corrupting God's attitudes to us with our own pathetic feelings. But there is no doubt about the centrality of love in God's dealings with humankind. This and other attitudes express most deeply the tenor of the relationship which God has with us. We in turn are called to love God with all our heart, soul, mind and strength, a complete response which captures our emotions in many ways. A Christian's praise to God will 'whoop it up', because flattery of the Creator is not possible and we cannot exaggerate God's glory and graciousness. Similarly, it is joy to suffer for the faith. Many of these emotions are relational. We are to live at peace with people, take delight in what is good in their lives, and live in hope with them.

But, further, our emotions play a score which is bigger than ourselves. The meaning of joy, peace, anger and hurt is set in the purposes of God. We are to love on God's terms, and anything else fails to respect and honour properly the person we love. We can, of course, go off and 'do our own thing', introducing dissonances into our relationships. We may not even hear when we are off pitch and out of tune. Yet the truth of our emotional life remains written in the great themes of the score. We learn these themes and grow into them as we play under the direction of the Composer. Our self-generated scrapings just do not make sense.

Thus Christianity not only affirms emotions but also confronts them with a critique. Emotions can be as wrong as actions, motives, injustice and hypocrisy. The biblical critique of emotions is both direct and very subtle. Lust, coveting, fear of others and envy are wrong, and are to be cut out of our lives. The Psalms repeatedly show strong emotions being disarmed by being set in a wider context, which is God's. Christianity also offers us an unconventional process of emotional retuning. We are to count it joy when we suffer for the good, because the power of evil is being challenged. Those who mourn are meeting truly what they face, and will be blessed.

Egocentric emotion

By contrast, humanism has in principle no critique of emotions. Whatever the egocentric human feels is valid, perhaps as long as it does not harm others. In (at least) the last two hundred years we have witnessed the gradual self-assertion of human emotions which are damaging and destructive. The dilemma is focused in the recent confession of a young man who murdered his girlfriend. He could only ask how he could come to kill the one he loved. The answer partly lies in the fact that emotions are permitted to be a law unto themselves – even the emotion called love. This occurs when emotions, instead of being rooted in our relationship with God, are turned in on our own egos. We are so often trapped in this situation that it is worth considering it at greater length.

38

First, the focus has changed. It is no longer an open relationship with God and the beloved that rules, but the subject's feelings. Indeed, the role of the other person is often to maintain the subject's desired emotional state. Her job is to make me feel in love, and if she does not allow me to stay in this blissful subjective state I am likely to be angry. So I ask this sensitive instrument to play only one note, which I like, rather than respond to the melody of the relationship. When the note does not sound right to me, I jump violently from one note to another, and fail to find the tune. The feelings vacillate between love and anger when real needs, weaknesses and hurts appear – as they must. The emotion is a tyrant that demands fulfilment. It knows no other sovereign claim; it will not bend to argument, to norms, to friendship or to persuasion. Although these responses are called feelings of love, they are actually always about *me*, and fundamentally exclude and dominate the very person I am supposed to be loving.

This then leads on to emotional blackmail. A couple is sensitive to each other's feelings. They can be picked up from a glance, the angle of the head or the way the door is closed. Yet it is easy to communicate a single emotional message: 'I want you to make me feel like this. I want peace and quiet. I want to be happy. I want to be sexually aroused.' Often these emotional requirements are accompanied by emotional threats. 'If you do not give me peace and quiet, I will be irritable and angry. If you do not make me happy, I will sulk. If you won't arouse me, I'll turn my back.' Thus, the egocentricity of the emotional requirements produces its own unsuitable pattern of threats and self-indulgence. Emotions fly around, creating havoc with relationships. It is still often called love, but the fruits show how far it is from the real thing.

John came in the door, muttered 'Hello', slung his case down and plonked himself in front of the television. His whole demeanour said, 'Leave me alone; I want a break.' Helen was silent for three minutes, and then told him that their son Peter was still not home. He was angry, and went out to the car before Helen could suggest where Peter might be. She was anxious, but it was still possible that he was coming back with his friend Bruce; she hadn't been able to leave two-year-old Fiona and find out. When Peter actually arrived home, she told him off more crossly than was justified. Eventually John came back, and told Helen off for not being firmer with Peter. The meal was not a pleasant one, and Fiona was throwing food at the cat again.

The self-referencing focus of emotions is often dangerous. Sometimes it forms a black hole into which the person disappears in depression or elation. We cannot conceive that the emotion might be wrong. Anger that is unjust and petulant, love that is misplaced and possessive, longing that is self-indulgent, or lust that is predatory is right 'because I feel it'. It must be followed through. It cannot be thought about, or morally guided. Much less can it be handed over to God for an overhaul and reassessment. At the same time, the feeling becomes unreal and artificial. Because the reference point has become egocentric, it is cut off from that which would generate its genuine expression. Then, because it is no longer spontaneous, we may need to manufacture it; and thus we become engaged in a process of self-manipulation in which the feeling of love is artificially stimulated. A comparable process takes place in the person who feels the need for sexual arousal, dissociates it from a real relationship, masturbates to engender the sexual feelings, and then feels the emptiness and loneliness of this disassociated act. The drive for pure feeling generates hollowness because it loses touch with what the meaning of the feelings must actually be. Shakespeare expressed the point in *Twelfth Night*:

> If music be the food of love, play on;
> Give me excess of it, that, surfeiting,
> The appetite may sicken, and so die.[6]

To feel 'in love' in this arbitrary emotional sense is also to fall out of it, and to be trapped in subjectivity. Thus self-governing emotion wreaks havoc in the human heart.

Autonomous emotion

The feeling of love has developed its own career in the twentieth century. When it becomes sovereign over relationships, a number of things happen. In the first stage, the feeling is allowed to override other norms; it is an excuse for not being patient and sensitive and for failing to show respect. Then, being in love takes primacy over marital faithfulness, and becomes an excuse for hurting and rejecting a husband or wife. The affair takes precedence over marriage, as it did with Byron and the Romantics, and as it now does with Hollywood, or (more mundanely) with the retreat from faithful love in millions of marriages. Being in love, in the sense of bowing to this feeling, is often accompanied by bullying. The boy creates pressure to go to bed by questioning the girl's love for him. Although the subject feels that this is love, in substance it is often worship of one's own feelings in a way that enslaves the other person. If couples were able to get rid of this emotional bullying, the stages of courtship would be more serene. But, instead, the problem develops. The feeling loses its inner meaning by becoming a perverted form of self-love, and must find a surrogate source of stimulation if it is to be maintained.

Simon wanted to go to bed with Jean. The need obsessed him and coloured all of his life, including the times he was with her. He could not sleep properly, and it was the hidden agenda whenever they met. She had slept with two other men, whom she had later come to dislike, and said she wasn't going through the same experience again. Simon was furious that two men had slept with her and he couldn't. He had actually played football against one of them on Saturday, and had temporarily enjoyed three very firm tackles. That evening, Jean said that unless they dropped the subject, the relationship was off. Simon frowned angrily all weekend, but on Sunday evening he calmed down and recognized that he loved Jean on the terms she had set. He phoned and apologized. As Jean said later, after that phone call the relationship had a chance.

Most serious is the use of the other person to experience this perverted emotion of feeling in love. The relationship then becomes tinged with or dominated by one partner's need for love. This is especially likely if the feelings left over from an earlier relationship are being resolved in this one. If I desperately need to be loved, I will find it very difficult to give love freely. Sometimes the feeling can move into fantasy. In that case, whether the stimulus is pornography, cheap novels or afternoon soap operas, feelings of 'love' float around in a state of detachment from any objective reality or any actual relationship. These feelings, though labelled 'love', turn out to be fantastic and destructive. Because the process is unreal, it is likely to end in emptiness and bitterness.

The development of this attitude might go some way to explain the horror of rape and marital violence. To be slaves to our emotions requires that they be followed and served. Gradually the demands grow, and the impossibility of meeting them generates tension. Self-control, and the integration of the emotions in a whole person, disappear. Acts are dictated by the rampant feeling which cannot be gainsaid, until the tyranny is imposed on a victim. Many media forms invite people to travel inside their emotions to the end of the line: states of fear, sexual intoxication, excitement and aggression are sought and achieved through horror movies, hard pornography, suspense thrillers and violent films. Financial rewards gained by the peddlers of this emotional garbage spur them on to generate more of it and thus to damage and ensnare the emotionally weak.

Being in love

Yet these patterns are far from the full picture. Being in love has an alternative pedigree, which comes from the Christian tradition. Here emotion plays a dignified part in defining what it means to be human, whether woman or man. Thinking, working, learning and worship are all threads in the emotional tapestry of life. And so is the feeling of love. Of course, love is not all feeling, nor is

emotion its core. What then is the feeling of love? It is
partly the desire fully to know and to be known by another
person, the desire for union, and the need to cherish this
special person. But this is more than emotion; it leads to
action, thought and talking. It is hung out on the other
person and remains relational. To revert to our earlier
metaphor, the emotions are the orchestra which plays the
score written by the relationship. To wait for her is to be
patient. To care is to worry when he is late. To know that
she is sleeping peacefully is joy. To find him overworked is
to be eager to help. To see her beauty is to be filled with a
sense of glory. The rich melody of emotions follows from
the relationship and from the object of love, and is bound
up with thought and action in a whole response. Whether it
is a feeling of *real* love depends on its truth or falsity. True
love strikes deeper than our moods; it is both the rhythm
of life and the changing tune. The actual relationship
imparts the emotional timbre. If the relationship is good,
the feelings will be good too, and *vice versa*. Feelings are
signals of our interpersonal sensitivity. When they go
wrong, they need to be heeded and shared, and examined
in the light of God's goodness and of the deeper meaning
of love, before they become unintelligible or out of control.

The meaning of the feelings, then – however over-
powering and glorious they are – lies beyond them. They
are a sign of what is so good and wonderful in the other
person. To snatch at the feelings without God is to pick the
flower and hold it without water.

Chapter 3

ROMANTIC LOVE

> They say love makes the world go round.
> They mean *our* love, I'm sure,
> For when we take a stroll, the ground
> Spins back round the earth's core.

The word 'romantic' is often used to express a certain kind of feeling, but in this chapter it is reserved for a view of love which is quite distinct from the popular usage. The feeling of love focuses on the subject's emotions; but this other meaning of romantic love focuses on the object – on the beloved as the one to be worshipped, the one who provides the meaning of life. This love is unself-conscious; it vests everything in the other person.

The true romantic relationship becomes central to life. Everything draws its meaning from the beloved and is tinted by the relationship. Young men will write her name in the most peculiar places simply because it should be there, and young women dream of him when typing a letter or cutting their toenails. It is perhaps particularly an experience of youth; the young person faces this other person for whom he or she would give everything. But the experience also engulfs many who are middle-aged and old. This kind of love has been around a long time, at least since, as legend has it, the beauty of Helen summoned Greece to fight the Trojan Wars and launched a thousand ships. It is great and magnificent. It is the Big One that provides the meaning of the universe and answers every question. It is the spindle of the wheel of life, the power for living, and dangerous stuff. It will ignore convention, riches, status and habit. To live for love and to find the heart of meaning in love is surely the answer which will carry everything before it. Looking into her eyes makes everything else fall into place. He knows that there is nothing she could ask of him that he would not do. As long as this is right, everything else will be right too.

People's reactions to romantic love differ. Some embark on a long quest for the person who will change the world. They train for the event with film stars, novels and people they worship from afar. When the person finally arrives, the relationship is all-engulfing. Others vaguely wish they or their spouses were more romantic. If only he would climb the drainpipe with a rose between his teeth instead of slouching in an armchair! Others, again, see romance as dangerous because it is all-consuming; they feel the need for a more controlled pattern of loving. Some think they have passed through this 'stage' and graduated to post-romantic relationships. They intend to have a much more matter-of-fact lifestyle, unentangled by other people. Some are angry that what they believed in turned out to be an illusion.

Few of us are untouched by this kind of love; but what it is remains an enigma.

A Christian interpretation of the core experience

There is something very important in the core experience of romantic love. Yet it is, perhaps, interpreted in the wrong terms. In this section we shall suggest a Christian slant on romantic love. First, the good part.

Many daily relationships are affected by social barriers, work, differences of attitude and the self-contained isolation which many people adopt to survive. Alongside this, really to meet someone is an awesome experience. Here is this person who is actually *with* me; it brings openness and transparency. Each of us at last feels fully human, and we know we can share ourselves without fear. There is an added glory when this kind of 'meeting' takes place between a woman and man. It mirrors the time in creation when God brought Eve to Adam, and the man let out a great hymn of response which marvelled that Eve was like him. He gave her a name which was like his name, and recognized in a fundamental sense that he was no longer alone – she was flesh of his flesh and bone of his bone. Shakespeare echoes this theme in *The Tempest*, when Miranda, having scarcely seen a man in her adult life, beholds Ferdinand. It is a point of wonder whenever woman meets man, because that meeting is basic to our human condition, expressing the sexual completeness of humankind as God has created us. This is deepened when each person gives herself or himself to the other, particularly when it includes the giving of themselves bodily, uncovering and sharing everything. There should be a sense of awe whenever a man and a woman come into union, when self-discovery goes along with giving one's whole self to the other person. This love, openness, intimacy, carefulness, sensitivity and total commitment make a union which involves everything: the way the partners act, think, eat, sleep, play and do the ironing. It is uninhibited, for everything goes into the commitment and nothing is held back. It is not circumstantial, but is for better or worse, for richer or poorer, in sickness and in health. This is what many people seek in romantic love, and it is wholly good. But it is not what romantic love means in our culture.

For this Christian understanding of husband–wife love, and of the wonder of all real relationships, is part of a wider truth. God's love is central to the creation of the universe and gives meaning to the life of every person and to every relationship. Love has its origin with God, and is reflected in the detailed care with which the creation is structured. It is expressed to us, in ways which we can readily understand, through Christ's life and teaching. God's commitment to us goes beyond our weakness and is the underlying reality of all our lives. And love is the norm by which God commands us to relate to one another, to our spouses and to God. It is the truth about our relationships whether we recognize it or not. This is the ultimate to which our finite love is a response. We are called to love

God (and one another) with all our heart, soul, mind and strength. Yet the rock-solid truth of God's love, the reliability of the terms in which it should be expressed, and its insistence on the need for honesty before God mean that this love does not die when we fail; it outlasts our pettiness and survives our failure. The meaning of love is given by God, reflects the character of God, and is written into the creation. Love exists on God's terms, and is exemplified by the conquering commitment of love in Jesus' life, despite the evil and failure to which he was subjected.

By contrast, romantic love seeks the meaning of love and of life in a particular, fallible human relationship. Such a view of love asks the partner to become god, an object of worship and a source of power. This no man or woman can do. Not surprisingly, therefore, the literary and actual history of romantic love has always been closely linked with tragedy. What seems so wonderful at the beginning turns into something which does not work. This meaning of love also turns it into an exclusive sexual form, which eradicates from people's consciousness love expressed in terms of friendship, family, community, church, work and nation. Romanticism has played a large part in excluding love from many areas of our lives.

Finally, the failures of romantic love have led millions of people into cynicism and mistrust; they are the post-romantics, the ones who will never again be taken in and who have closed themselves to the true meaning of love. The cost of these romantic failures has been great, despite the great optimistic belief of romantic love that nothing but good can come from it. Before we examine these in detail, it is worth looking at the history of Romanticism to see how it has developed away from Christianity to become a faith in itself.

The history of romantic love

Perhaps the modern European expression of romantic love begins with the medieval code of courtly love. The gallant knight pursued an adoring and inspiring relationship with a chaste and unattainable woman. Adoration of her inspired his noble acts, but the relationship either remained unrequited or could not be consummated. We find this theme in the *Legend of Arthur and the Round Table*, *The Romance of the Rose* and other great medieval literature. In Italy this tradition developed with two great heroic relationships, those of Dante and Beatrice and Petrarch and Laura. Dante met the girl he celebrates as 'Beatrice' when they were children. She married someone else and died as a young woman, but nevertheless became the inspiration of Dante's life and work. In his greatest work, the *Divine Comedy*, the blessed spirit of Beatrice guides him through Paradise. Petrarch continued to worship the woman he calls Laura before and after her death in his poetry and writing. Laura and Beatrice were seen as the inspirers of all that was good. Later, as more secular, humanistic attitudes spread through Italy, thousands copied the idea of the woman as the object of worship and the inspiration of life. Today we experience it most directly in opera when a tenor sings of his love for the heroine.

The idea took another form during the Renaissance. The old Greek and Roman gods and goddesses were revived, not to be worshipped as deities, but to embody human hopes and possibilities. Venus was rediscovered. The painter Botticelli, in one of his most famous works, painted her drifting in on a seashell as a mythic alternative to the creation of Eve. Other painters portrayed Venuses who happened to be their mistresses or patrons. One painting by Titian shows a man playing a keyboard while gazing at his prostrate Venus; the painting implies that she is the inspiration for his music. The idea of the grand passion, which was usually extramarital, took root in Italian culture. This Renaissance idea spread through much of Europe. The worship of female beauty as an ultimate focus became deeply embedded in male culture.

The all-consuming relationship between hero and heroine lifted men and women above the merely mortal. In England its most famous development is in Shakespeare's work, especially his tales of Romeo and Juliet, Antony and Cleopatra, and Othello and Desdemona. Heroic love in this sense became important throughout much of Europe. In

England, however, this tradition waned under the influence of alternative Christian views which gave room for passion within marriage and saw adultery as betrayal.

Only in the late eighteenth century did modern Romanticism really begin, probably as a result of the Enlightenment – the cultural movement which established humanity as the focus of worship. The earlier, dominant attitude of this period (for the men) was to hold the world and relationships at a distance, and to try to understand them 'rationally'. Towards the end of the eighteenth century, this approach failed. Contradictory views of reason arose, and reached widely varying conclusions. People suddenly began to look for a different way of approaching the world, embracing it and identifying their souls with it. A sense of empathy with nature, with the past, or even with the nation, became the inspiration of life. Above all, the total unification of the soul with the beloved became the central reality around which all else was seen to revolve.

At its heart, Romanticism involved a new hope for identity. To be at one with nature, or with the past, or with the beloved, was the meaning of life and of love. The quest of the soul for wholeness was a movement which swept through Europe. The figures of the Romantic movement are well known – Goethe, Schiller, Wordsworth, Beethoven, Shelley, Byron, Delacroix and Keats, to name a few. They were all involved in the great transition which is summed up in the legend of Faust. They were turning their backs on God, whatever the consequences, and seeking the one thing which would give their lives meaning. In Goethe's *Faust*, the hero's quest is not for pleasure, wealth or learning, but for love. The love he finds is actually the love of a Christian woman, but the terms he negotiated with Mephistopheles mean that he must find in it the meaning of his life. Faust's love for Margarete is an act of identification. 'Henceforth,' he says, 'be our whole being lost in one another in overflowing joy – that lives and lives for ever and for ever.' But the tragedy of choosing to play Mephistopheles' game works its way through to damnation.

For Wordsworth, similarly, identification with nature gives intimations of immortality. He sees the daffodils, and pow! he is at one with the universe. At the centre of these romantic experiences was the idea that the human spirit could meet that with which it could identify, and which would mirror back its true self. This was the era of national anthems; people felt an identity with their nation which gripped their guts and claimed their lives. It was also the era when Byron made the pilgrimage back to ancient Greece, and the Arthurian legends wrung the hearts of the English. Although there were natural, national and historical forms of Romanticism, however, the most dominant home for the spirit was in the arms of the beloved. This was where identity was discovered and where a man's soul ended its quest. Spiritual union with the beloved was the point of life.

Yet this new meaning of love seemed always to lead to tragedy. Goethe's *The Sorrows of Young Werther* told how the emotion of love and the misunderstanding of society drove the young hero to suicide; from then on many a hand-wringing hero and heroine hung on to a romantic love tinged with sadness. Shakespeare's great romantic tragedies were rediscovered and played to full Victorian houses with great pathos. The German composers wrote *Leider* which extolled this great emotional reality and which were sung around the piano in Victorian homes. It is easy to forget how seriously the Victorians took this angst of the heart, and how exalted was their vision of romantic love and of tragedy. In Germany at the same time, Wagner's Siegfried and Brunhild repeatedly expired to deep sighs from the audience. This sense of tragedy seems to have arisen from an awareness that somehow this love could not bear the weight upon it; people desperately wanted it to succeed, but it cracked and was not enough. As a religion, romantic love was inadequate.

Soon the seriousness gave way. Later, popular, romantic songs with more vulgar themes were sung in the music halls. 'Sentiment' became one of the great characteristics of late nineteenth-century life. 'Daisy, Daisy, . . . on a bicycle made for two' requires a well-lubricated throat to carry conviction. At the end of the century, other developments, more obsessive and destructive, grew out of the dynamics of romantic love.[1] Many became much more sceptical as the First World War, poverty and revolution besmirched this rosy view of life.

In the twentieth century, Romanticism has been revived by Hollywood. The romantic film pulled in the crowds. It obviously spoke to the yearnings of the young people who flocked to the cinemas. Everywhere the message was that when the two hearts were united, everything would be fine: Charlie Chaplin and his girl strolled off into the sunset, and all was well. Hollywood constructed male and female stars who could be adored by the opposite sex. Women swooned when their man came on the screen, and men silently worshipped as every film of their idol appeared. Perhaps someone like this idol lived round the corner. Sure enough, girls round the corner began to look and dress like the idols!

Through the middle decades of this century, the idols became more sexual and physical – Mary Pickford, Jane Russell, Marilyn Monroe, Brigitte Bardot on the one hand and Charlie Chaplin, Gary Cooper, Robert Redford and Arnold Schwarzenegger on the other. They became the Venuses and Apollo's of the twentieth century. Mainly outside Hollywood, the film industry developed its own anti-romantic anti-heroes, but even as this was happening the old films were travelling round the world winning new converts to Romanticism. In India, romantic love communicated through films has taken a complete culture by storm in less than two decades. The often unthinking transmission of Romanticism became a self-perpetuating industry, with newspapers spitefully pointing out the contrast between the idols' screen lives and real lives (Antony and Cleopatra were Richard Burton and Elizabeth Taylor), while feeding off Romanticism at the same time. The inconsistency of media responses to Charles and Diana reflects this very process. On the one hand, then, romantic love has been promoted by the media on an unprecedented scale; while on the other a vast underworld of anti-romantic feeling has developed. It is difficult for anyone to escape being romantic and cynical at the same time.

The fatal flaw

The early Romantics, such as Byron, Shelley and Wordsworth, knew that they were creating an alternative religion. Worship was being transferred from God to a man or a woman under the name of love, which was seen as a source of salvation and identity. The dynamics of this kind of relationship need exploring, because they are very complicated. The analysis includes understanding what it is like to be a god or a goddess. Humanism transfers the central meaning of life from God to human beings, so that they become gods and goddesses in their own right. Yet gods and goddesses, even small ones, must have a glory which has no outside source; they produce good vibrations and are to be served; they are by definition good, and they are the focus of all that exists. To fall in love in these terms is to bow the knee and submit: La Belle Dame sans Merci hath thee in thrall. Sometimes people aspire to this kind of status; it seems quite an attractive existence. More often, it is a mantle draped over their shoulders by their partner. Yet it weighs terribly heavily.

It is easy to suppose that there are few gods and goddesses walking around; most people do not look grand enough. But this is to miss the point. All that one ordinary person needs in order to slip into the role is a single worshipper. Some become gods by emphasizing how important their time is; they are about their business and nothing is to be allowed to distract them. Some of us develop an aura which says how special we are. Not a few women believe that it is a privilege for a man to take them out and pay the bills. Thousands of trivial activities establish patterns which convey how important, how beautiful, how infallible, some people are. Yet it would be a mistake to assume that all these attitudes always involve *self*-glorification. A wife may commit herself fully to her husband's career; she supports it and to some extent lives vicariously in it. He genuinely wants to succeed 'for her sake'. Things go wrong, but the couple suffer beyond the circumstances because both had built on this kind of glory.

Those who feel the need to inspire their partners are just ordinary people. But they must behave as if they were always in control or as if their beauty captivated. Perhaps they are never allowed to make mistakes. What they say must always be the last word: '"Let spades be trumps!" she said, and trumps they were.' Perhaps they always have to be served, and are never allowed to lift a finger for themselves or for anybody else. Whatever frailties there are must remain hidden so as not to undermine the terms on which the relationship is set up. This is a very lonely existence. A person who is worshipped can never become dependent on a spouse without breaking the structure of the relationship. Our culture, by encouraging us to build upon images of intelligence, strength, beauty, power and charisma, trains us to be mini-gods and mini-goddesses. When these images have this false principle behind them, they shrink those who dwell inside them, even colouring all that is good in their lives.

Megan had worked with Roger for thirteen years and knew everything about him. He had done good work, had a deservedly high reputation and was always in demand. Everybody in the office and at home depended on him. He had worked so hard. Now the orders had tailed off and the work had dwindled. He had cancer – probably not terminal – and his treatment began next week. Megan had discussed it carefully with his wife Nancy, although neither was supposed to know of his illness. She knew that at 2:30 this afternoon he would have no work to do. At 2:25 she asked if he wanted coffee, and brought it through. He looked defeated in his chair; she hovered slightly and asked him if he was unwell.

'No, I'm fine.'

She swallowed hard and said quietly, 'No, you are not. I've talked to Nancy and she knows you have cancer, and we've discussed how we can help you.'

In half a second the armour of professional competence fell away; he smiled, then laughed, thanked her and phoned home.

53

Thus anybody who tries to be a god or a goddess must be alone. But there are other costs. When the god fails, the worshipper is let down. The god should offer salvation in material, sexual or emotional terms, and has failed to do so. This comes as a crisis of faith which overturns everything. When the girl who has made life radiant does not do so any more, she is punished. When the woman who can do no wrong does wrong, it seems unforgivable. When the man who is in control fails, he cannot be trusted with anything. Sometimes, before this happens, the person is aware of its likelihood and retreats to the safety of a pedestal, and so distance replaces the ordinary intercourse of two open people. When a young woman marries an older man, his maturity and *savoir-faire* may put him in an elevated position. He may even have been her boss at work. He is in control and knows the score. Then both of them grow older. She gains the experience to question what he says and does. If he feels threatened by this and hangs on to his godlike status rather than accepting the change as a normal part of maturing, there is trouble.

Of course, none of us believes that we are *fully* gods and goddesses; we are omniscient only in some areas, and our self-importance knows some boundaries. Even so, millions of men and women wear the crestfallen expression of fallen idols. They may have been put on a pedestal by their partners, or they may have climbed up there themselves, but it has eventually keeled over. Like Dagon, the idol of the Philistines, there is no way it can ever be erected again.

Nor is the position any better for the worshipper. He or she hangs everything on this relationship. Without it the worshipper does not exist, and even its limited failure threatens annihilation. In *Anna Karenina*, Tolstoy depicts the terrible dynamics of this process. Anna leaves her husband and even her son for the compelling love of Vronsky, on which she hangs her life. But soon Vronsky is not able to bear the weight, and seeks to create his own space in quite ordinary ways. Anna finds that this threatens the central meaning of her life, and seeks to bind Vronsky in her total love. At the same time she begins to become aware of his limitations and faults, and these anger her so that she repeatedly rows with him. Gradually the fragile basis of her total commitment is exposed; her life is left without meaning, and she finally throws herself under a train. Sometimes a situation occurs where both partners are so dependent on each other for their identity that the relationship collapses. They cannot grow in normal healthy ways, because the only meaning they have is in their romantic love. Gudrun and Gerald exemplify this in D. H. Lawrence's *Women in Love*.

In pursuit of this pattern, a woman might live vicariously through her husband. His work shapes her life. He requires the total sublimation of all she might want. All her emotions are subjected to his emotions. This situation, even if it occurs in a less extreme form, is unstable. Either she will eventually discover her feelings and thoughts, and move out of this pattern, probably with a few rows and traumas; or he, because he is relating to a no-one, will seek variety by continually provoking her or by finding somebody else. Worshippers are often walked over by petty gods. But many worshippers are dishonest. They see through the gods whom they have served, and continue only with a semblance of worship. They sing a hymn once a week and then go about their normal business. They have seen through romantic love, and, in dismissing it, believe that they have said goodbye to the possibility of love at all.

Popular romantic love

Today, romantic love is more mundane. Women are given irresistible power by their perfume, or men by designer clothes. The flattery which generates self-importance is daily performed by the advertising industry. The New Age movement tells us we are all gods and goddesses, and can engage in self-worship. Millions of us practise being little bronzed gods and goddesses on crowded beaches each summer. It is nice to receive even a little lukewarm idolatry; wouldn't it be fun to be adored by women or to be a *femme fatale*? No longer do most men believe that the meaning of life can be found in a relationship with a woman, but they might be happy to settle for the meaning of the next few months.

Each new generation arrives at adulthood with some version of the doctrine of romantic love. Those who have experienced little love in their own families, or for whom work is tedious, are deeply tempted to see in romantic love a blinding and total solution to life. The young woman finds an older man who lifts her from inattention to being an object of worship. It is wonderful. The flattery works for a while, as the man knows it will; and then he moves on, manipulating the idiom of romantic love without an ounce of the stuff in his soul. She slowly regains her sight and loses her ability to open herself to her beloved. Boys and girls yearn to be idols who will command this kind of worship; it seems to be the only viable way of finding love. They dissect the lifestyle of the famous, searching for the formula which they in turn must adopt. Possessing a certain brand of trainers assumes unfathomable importance because of its necessary contribution to the desired self-image.

The popular forms of idolatry are very constricting, like the hourglass figure of the 1950s which the woman worthy of adulation had to squeeze herself into. The irresistible beauty spends hours applying make-up to achieve that status. Since Charles Atlas's body-building claims, the male equivalent has also been around. This pattern expresses an almost universal law. Those who seek to become idols are enslaved to them. The idioms turn out to be vain. They fundamentally mis-state who we are, and identify love with a particular kind of pretence and flattery. We play the games of romantic love, but know underneath that they are not true; this is not what we are really like.

Samantha found that Donald flooded her with attention. The contrast with being ignored at home, and with the customers who looked only at the banknotes she counted out, was vivid. She especially liked clothes-shopping together, so that he could tell her what looked best on her. They had a really good time, and she felt more confident; she swung her hair and took a longer stride. But after a while something went wrong. It was partly money; she was spending a lot, and Donald was spending even more on her. One afternoon the focus was so much on her and on what clothes she should buy that she tried to provoke him; he finished up buying an expensive dress that she did not really like. She was so angry, instead of grateful, that she left for home as quickly as possible and did some housework. Gradually the relationship fizzled out. Samantha suspected that Donald was a bit relieved, although he still said how much he adored her.

The deepest cost of Romanticism lies in the fact that it causes millions to give up on love. If this great love is supposed to be the meaning of life, what happens when it fails? If this person should inspire love, what if he or she fails? Because there seems to be nothing more, even the very young turn their backs on love. They fall passionately in love, experience some exploitative sex, and back off into wary relationships and post-romantic cynicism. They are unable to consider that the kind of love they trusted was fatally flawed. By contrast, we walk in a broad place when we open our lives to the scrutiny of God's love, so that our failures can be recognized for what they are and cleansed out of our relationships. We might be tempted to live in relationships of make-believe, supposedly inspiring love in each other; but the kind of love we need is that which recognizes and abides through our weaknesses and sin. That love cannot be disillusioned, because in principle it has no illusions.

Chapter 4

LOVE AS DUTY

For many, the prime conception of love is as duty. Women, especially in eastern societies, have been taught that it is their duty to love their husbands. At its most extreme in the past, this conception was demonstrated by the custom of suttee, whereby widows committed themselves to their husbands' funeral pyres. Now it is expressed in much more moderate ways. Dating agencies have recently done a strong trade in providing wives from Asia to husbands who dislike the emancipated western woman and prefer women who know what duty and submission mean. But the conception is not limited to the wife's duty to her husband, for Asian marriage also involves a strong understanding of the husband's duty to provide for his wife and children in economic circumstances which make that task a great sacrifice and endless hard work. By contrast, many western marriages seem flabby in their emphasis on self-gratification. Often the idea of duty is given strong religious sanction, with punishment or dishonour following failure to live in the prescribed way. In this study we shall not examine these eastern meanings, important though they are; but shall focus on duty in the West, a rather different idea.

Many western couples have experienced the pull of romantic love as a threat to their marriages, but duty has won and has re-established stability. Similarly, when emotions are running rife and creating chaos, sober duty can often restore order. Duty also provides strong subsidiary ideas. Love is seen as bringing home a wage, cooking his meals, having his shirts ironed or saying it with flowers. Indeed, when this pattern is changed, it can seem devastating.

When the wife says, 'No meal tonight; cook it yourself!' he knows something is wrong.

It is important not to parody this position or to under-estimate its strength and the compelling power it possesses. Unlike the positions we have previously examined, this one always provides an answer. Keep on doing your duty. Love your man or your woman. More than this, it has a hook on a central biblical truth. Love lasts; all these other things will vanish away, but love will never end. If love means being faithful, providing food and shelter for the family and never being angry, then you just get on and do these things in all circumstances. It also emphasizes putting the needs and problems of others before one's own. This commit-ment to giving priority to others provides the inner strength of many families and cannot be overvalued. Especially when one's spouse has turned out to be a despic-able heap, the 'duty' view of love sees the problem through. But in many relationships these views of duty are mixed up with others which are more questionable.

Love as morality

The meaning of duty is complex. One strand within it is the idea of love as doing good to the other person. The beloved receives cups of tea in bed or is given lavish presents, but behind these actions is the understanding that from good only good can come. The evidence is con-vincing, and for much of the time these household acts of care betoken love in a straightforward and heartwarming way.

Yet it is not quite so simple. It depends on the focus. If these actions have their focus in the lover rather than the beloved, they are acts of self-righteousness and self-justification rather than of love. There are a number of tests of this tendency. If past acts are brought up as a way of rebuking the partner or of justifying one's own actions, they are being woven into this fabric. If the other person feels done good to rather than really helped, the same is possibly going on. And if individuals cannot receive love and care without feeling insecure and slightly threatened,

THE MEANINGS OF LOVE

it is probable that they are trying to keep their bank of goodness fuller than anyone else's. Being good and doing good in a self-validating way are among the most powerful human motives, and few of us are immune to them. That is why Jesus criticized them so rigorously.

This can be accompanied by a kind of rigidity. Many of us have fixed views of the terms on which we will receive love from others. The checklists are often quite extra-ordinary. The man should dress in a certain way. The woman should be colour-coordinated. He should never be so rude as to disagree with her. She should always laugh at his jokes. He should never go to sleep in a chair. She should never break wind. Many of us have this detailed morality of loving because we value our loving so highly. Actually, our conception is built up from our parents, friends and culture and often reflects narrow views of love. Some people are very confident about the kind of love they offer and expect; they dictate the terms, and their partners are expected to fit in with them. Others are more circum-spect about the terms on which they give love; it even makes them timid. Early in a relationship, there is often a lot of anxiety attached to these moral codes. This reflects the extent to which we give and experience judgment on the kind of love which is acceptable.

Penny was so concerned about how she should dress for her date with David that she was an hour late. He had gone, and when she eventually caught up with him, the cinema was so dark that he scarcely saw her anyway. Queuing for the ice-cream took twenty minutes, and when they parted rather quickly afterwards, she worked out that he had seen her for only five minutes after two hours of getting ready. After that she eased up a bit when she went out.

Is my love good enough?

Linked with the moralism of love is the attitude which decides either to accept love or to reject it as not good enough. We shall call it the *probationary* attitude to love. Its effect on the other person is deep and debilitating. Will my love come up to scratch? Many children have a deep and haunting memory that the love they offered to their parents, brothers, sisters and friends was not good enough; it has been rejected. Thus the most valuable thing that they have to offer, their very being, is sent back as not good enough. Possibly they are asked to resubmit with improved performance. They learn that love means fulfilling certain conditions which will be acceptable to others. So they no longer give themselves, but work at the moral prerequisites which are necessary for acceptable love. The idea of 'moral' in this situation can amount to almost anything. A woman must accept physical violence or sexual abuse. A man must provide a home, decorations, furniture and a garden which are luxurious and perfect before his wife accepts that he really loves her. Each year he winces as the specification of what he must provide is pushed higher and he remains on probation. Or the woman believes she is loved on the grounds that she is an exciting person, and the worry sets in that if she changes, love will be withdrawn.

Whether one's love is good enough is a devastating question. Of course, proposals of marriage are refused, and friendships break down, but far deeper is the question whether love which is offered with a sincere heart is judged and rejected. Those who stand in judgment over such love with this kind of moral authority immediately have great power; they have the ability to make any situation into an examination where they will set the questions, mark the papers and decide the criterion by which one passes or fails. These judgments shape many love relationships, leaving one or both partners focusing critically on the performance and validity of the other's love in a way which must drive them apart from one another.

For this kind of approach must generate criticism, accusations and dissatisfaction. It contains an arrogance which says, 'I deserve such-and-such a kind of love, and you are so much less than I deserve.' The sense of self-rightness becomes self-righteousness as one partner evaluates the most precious thing that the other can give, concluding that it is not up to the mark. Holding this moral position can be used to induce a kind of perpetual slavery and a deep discouragement in the life of the other person. Love becomes an external performance which must come up to a certain standard before it is accepted. The heart has gone out of it and only a sense of behavioural failure is left.

A frequent response to this kind of moralism is for each partner to judge the other for the shortcomings of the love which is offered. Charge and counter-charge are presented in ways which aim to shift the weight of blame and moral failure to the other. In this kind of argument and quarrelling, each partner focuses on his or her own perceived strengths and locates the weaknesses of the other, so that moral superiority can be established. The arguments which each partner uses may have some validity, but the problem lies in the fact that the context is moralism, blame and self-righteousness, rather than love and openness. Behind the arguments lies the sense of hurt arising from the way their love has been judged, and an inability to respond positively. Couples in this situation will complain that the love has gone out of their marriage, which is quite accurate. It has been replaced by a pharisaic moralism which makes the giving and receiving of love impossible. This is constructed not only out of judgment, but also out of a refusal to recognize how hurtful attitudes and actions have been. The idea that 'it is not my problem' can be used as moral insulation. The only things that matter are who is right, and parrying blame.

Alison felt that she had an unbearable load. With the work and the children she had to organize the whole day down to the last minute. Dominic didn't pull his weight. What upset her most was the fact that he took time to relax and rest when she was tearing about. Because she was under pressure, she couldn't do things well. It was becoming worse because the children didn't help much either, even with a lot of nagging. Jason, Lucy and Tim were old enough to lend a hand, but they never seemed to know what to do, and everything fell on Alison's shoulders. She was the only one who knew how to do jobs properly. Nobody else had learned what housework involved. They were just as irresponsible as the

62

people at work. When Jason told her one day that she never *allowed* anybody to do anything, Alison exploded. But when the steam had cleared, she began to dish out tasks for the others to take on permanently, and was surprised, when they had learned to do them, how willingly and well they cooperated.

One of the astonishing things about Jesus is the way he broke through this moralistic garbage. First of all he firmly rejected all the judgments of himself, his disciples and those he met which arose from this assumed right to judge. When Martha chided Mary for not helping with the housework, he commended Mary for her commitment to learning and gave Martha space to cool down. He refused to allow his disciples to be censored for picking grain on the Sabbath, or children for shouting in the temple area. He turned the focus on the judgers, asking them to notice the planks in their own eyes before focusing on the speck in someone else's. He accepted people where they were; he recognized that people wanted him for the bread, the miracles, the healing and the excitement, but he always received whatever love was offered him. It came from a prostitute who was polluting him with her hair and tears; from a leper who said 'thank you' when he was healed; from a thief who was about to die. The love was often tested in straightforward ways, but always Jesus accepted what people gave of themselves without any of the burdens and provisos which those who were not the Son of God felt compelled to add. The central truth is that God is always able to relativize the performance in the light of our circumstances and situation; what he seeks is an open, loving heart and sincere commitment. A bruised reed he will not break and a slowly burning candle he will not blow out. Nor should we.

Love and duty through history

The language of duty has deeply affected love down the centuries, but it has taken a number of markedly different forms. One of the most influential is the Enlightenment conception of *rights*. It saw people as being born with certain natural rights, such as the life, liberty and pursuit of happiness of the American Declaration of Independence. Although these rights might signal important external constraints on others, for those who 'possessed' them they gave rise to a problem. They were self-regarding. My rights were what I could lay claim to. This code of thinking has deeply influenced the culture of love.

Within marriage it has normally reflected a breakdown in cooperation and a legalistic view of relationships. In English law, until as recently as 1991, a man had the implicit right to rape his wife whenever he felt like insisting on sex. Far more 'normal' is the plethora of customary rights which husbands always and wives more recently have insisted are part of their lot.

Many of the older patterns convey the idea of *territory* which was built into this approach. The husband had the right to leave the the kids with the wife. The wife had the right to collect the wages on pay-day and give him an allowance, or to collect him from the pub while he was still sober. The husband could throw the meal in the back of the fire if it was not up to scratch and demand that another be cooked. 'I know my rights!' was the war-cry in the trench warfare which occurred in many homes of the past.

The language of rights has changed, but it is just as common. Now, however, it focuses more fully on individual freedom – to spend, to enjoy a certain lifestyle, to pursue sexual adventure and to ignore the partner. The key to this approach is the justification it offers for whatever the individual wants, irrespective of the needs, concerns and fears of the partner. It is a form of systemized insensitivity in which each person becomes convinced of the right to go his or her own way regardless.

Another conception of duty was as *an act of the will*, often dissociated from emotion and understanding. It owes much to the philosopher Kant, and to the dualism which he built into his interpretation of human beings. On the one hand, the mind gathered ordered, rational knowledge of the external world; and on the other, the person exercised his will, guided by universal moral commands.[1] Love, since it was obviously not a matter of knowledge, was therefore a matter of will and duty. And Kant lived like that; people put their clocks right by the time at which he passed the door. This view had widespread influence; it was not uncommon for conversion to Christianity to be presented as an act of the will, with the assumption that emotion and understanding would follow. The moralism which was so pervasive in the nineteenth century was heavily influenced by views similar to Kant's. Love was a matter of deciding what was right and of carrying it out with an inner determination to see it through.

Where duty fails

This idea tends to see love as *impersonal*. It is universal in the sense that 'loving' is what one does to anybody. It involves establishing a rule which defines right conduct and then carrying it out as an act of the will. The conception of the love is contained in an armoured decision inside one person, and whoever receives the love is in a certain sense irrelevant. Recipients feel they are being done good to, but the love does not touch them personally, because it has nothing to do with them, but only with general concepts like soldiering on, doing right by people and being a good husband. It is an approach which is much comforted by rules. When the subject of love comes up, such a person is likely to respond, 'Well, I do this, that and the other; what more can I do?'

This kind of love is also impersonal with respect to the giver, because it leaves very little room for receiving love, for being the object of affection. Perhaps the lover is wary of being dependent on the love of others; perhaps she fears blame, or perhaps he just delights in following rules. The motives can vary, but if the point of generation is 'the will', there are likely to be problems. Sometimes people think that 'emotions' are unreliable and the 'will' trustworthy, but the exercise of the will often ignores and sublimates an emotional life which also needs to be addressed in terms of love. Only when our whole self is behind the chosen path is love pure and uncomplicated.[2]

'Stiff-upper-lip' types feel insecure on emotional ground and will try to make sure that relationships do not stray there.

A further sense of duty is *task-oriented*. It sets goals and ends which are seen as central to the business of loving. Indeed, some people approach loving like a business operation. Then, when the goals are fulfilled, love will have been done. The lady receives a fur coat or a new house, and the lover either sets himself a new task or sits back and congratulates himself on a task completed. Because the sense of love is always based on activity, it then becomes difficult to give love in any other terms – through listening, suffering, accepting or waiting. This view always looks to the future; it is doing things for next week or next year. The relationship which takes place in the present is a working one, but it does not allow the couple to down tools.

Fred and Freda were both in the green movement. They had met clearing a river north of London. When they were married, Fred committed himself to creating the best home he could for Freda. He worked hard; they moved twice and within four years had a fine home in Twickenham.

On Christmas Day in the fifth year a number of things struck them. The first was the cooking. Because Fred had worked so hard to make home into the place Freda would enjoy, she had responded by doing more and more elaborate cooking. It seemed to fit the home. But previously, they had liked plain, simple food. Second, there was the question of children. Now that they had sorted out the house, they were ready for children. They had talked the agenda through many times before, but it was all too neat; it seemed to be making life into just one thing after another. Finally, there was ecology. Without wanting to do so, they were moving into being big consumers. Life was running them.

After church, they had a light snack and then went for a long walk through the deserted streets of London, and it was on that walk that their love dived beneath these self-imposed pressures into something more tranquil.

Often, however, it is not those who live by duty who are the source of the problem, but those who set up the dutiful patterns. If the husband's career requires it, then of course it is the wife's duty to move yet again; should any other possibility receive consideration? Those who receive dutiful love can even abuse the person who is giving it (especially since they may feel they have a vested interest in reinforcing the pattern) by nagging, the use of financial power, physical violence, moral blackmail or frequent appeal to a sense of duty which they themselves ignore. By using this view of love, millions (mainly men) have heaped untold suffering on their spouses. Wives have cowered under drunken men in the name of duty. Partners have sobbed themselves to sleep at the unfaithfulness of their mates, hanging on to the thin thread of duty. Men have humoured extravagant wives, buttressed by a sense of duty.

There is something degenerate going on here. The idea of duty is imposed on a person who is then to be treated without dignity, respect or affection. In the past, especially, some women have been left with all the repetitive and uninteresting jobs, while the men have lived more exciting lives. Some of those men have then found their dutiful wives boring. The problem, normally, is not so much with the dutiful wives as with the husbands who create dutiful wives by expectations and grumbling. Those who find their partners uninteresting have probably made them that way by closing down possibilities of communication and action. No person is boring, but lack of care and sensitivity pushes the partner into routine and predictable responses, often with a deep awareness of how far from real love and concern his or her life is being lived.

The baddies and the goodies

Deep within this meaning of love is the idea of *being good enough to be loved*. Many people are crushed by what they consider as failure, measured by some of the standards set out above. They have not done well in their careers, or they are unemployed, and they feel deeply that they have let down the one they love. They have been unable to give their partners what is seen as a basic right. So, for example, many of the 10% or so of couples who are unable to give birth to children add to their disappointment the completely unwarranted feeling that they are letting each other down. Other people are aware of characteristics in themselves which they feel are despicable and make them failures and unworthy of love. It may be past sexual relationships or the way they have treated their parents and brothers and sisters. Many suffer from addictions which give them a sense of repeated failure.

Often, however, the problem lies not in anything they have done, but in the attitudes of others. Children become discouraged when they are described to their faces in ways which imply they will never change. 'There's no hope for him.' These assessments, which may be fed even by mild criticisms, paralyse the ability of many people to love. They have an overwhelming sense of how little value their love must have. This is crushing, especially when conveyed to the young child by the parent. The sense of defeat makes all attempts at love half-hearted. 'We have failed before, so surely we shall do so again.' What seems like an inability to love is likely to stem from lack of confidence. The answer to it is straightforward and fills the New Testament. The heartfelt love of each person is of inestimable value. We do fail in our love, as Peter did when he denied Christ. But we can be forgiven; we can recover and learn to love better. Those who turn their backs on the love of others do not know God.

There is another devastating effect of this sense of failure; people withdraw, feeling that nobody could love them if they revealed what they are truly like. They retain a private area where skeletons remain hidden. This move has peculiar consequences.

First, it is likely to mean that the 'true self', which superficial onlookers do not see, is the failure. It becomes central to a person's identity and it is the thing that he or she cannot talk about to anybody. Even more incongruous is the fact that many of the sources of failure – childhood and adult abuse, educational barriers, lack of skills, physical and health problems – are not the fault of the person who experiences them so deeply as failure.

Second, this sense of being a failure leads the person to dismiss the love of others, because it is seen as being based on a misconception. 'If only they knew me as I am, they would not love me any more.' The wars which take place in people's hearts because of this are titanic. On the one hand, they are in love and want to open up their lives to their beloved. On the other hand, maybe during the early stages of friendship, they presented themselves to their love in a favourable light, and now the last thing they want is to reveal the failures and sense of unworthiness which dwell in their lives. They hug with one arm and keep their partner at arm's length with the other. With care and patience, all these areas of failure, sin and unworthiness, if they matter at all, can be brought out of privacy into a relationship where love removes the fear which made them grow.

Those whose sense of love is marked by self-approval, however, have a greater problem. They are doing it right, or have marked out their daily ration of love. It involves taking the children to school, washing up after supper and putting the cat out, plus shopping on Fridays. It is the love which tots up all it has done in the last month. Like the Pharisee in the parable, who prayed with himself listing all he did and thanking God that he was not like 'this publican', this kind of love is only involved in a dialogue with itself. Whatever good is done is not done in relationship, but performed in front of the mirror. It is felt by others as external, and does not touch them where they are. It brings destructive self-congratulation into what is supposed to be love, and spreads a sense of failure through people's lives. Instead of meeting one another face to face, people pass one another dressed in their own petty notions of what love should be like. The care with which Jesus attacked this attitude shows that it must be one of the most potent sources of bondage in human lives. The goodies and the baddies do not exist.

Love and grace

Too often in the past, duty and moralism have been identified as a Christian view of love. They are not, and the Bible steadfastly criticizes all views which seek to identify good and moral behaviour with human judgments and standards. When the focus is on human valuations of love, then people begin to stand over the law of love and make it their own, and to interpret it as a method of bringing others to account. This kind of pride immediately subverts the true meaning of love and turns it into a weapon of blame and recrimination. Jesus' criticisms of the destructive, burdensome nature of this approach to love ring out through the gospels, and Paul makes clear that all self-centred attempts at love which have as their agenda the rightness of the individual are doomed. The only hope is to move into the enjoyment of God's love – a love which is not an individual act of the will, but which encompasses the whole relationship in grace.

God's grace is not a matter of desert or of earning capacity, but begins with the free, undeserving commitment of God to us as persons. As Jesus took Peter through his multiple failures into the ability to love and give, so we are invited on the same journey. It offers us no hope of resting in our duty, goodness or rights, but instead validates our ability to respond to God and to love one another, however pathetic our present abilities. These relationships penetrate far deeper than rule-oriented behaviour which locks on to individual performance. They reach into our failures and successes and put both in a bigger context. They keep the focus of the relationship open instead of self-regarding.

Damion could not cope. He had been unfaithful to his wife, Mary. It was casual sex over a weekend when he was away and got drunk. He knew he had to tell Mary. At first he argued to himself that because it was casual, it need not matter to either of them; but then he saw how that cheapened his participation in their own love-making, and fortunately he dropped that line quickly. Then he focused on what he had done. There were no excuses; it was despicable. Mary would be right to blame him. The most pathetic thing was to have had sex with another woman while Mary was pregnant. Damion rehearsed all the things Mary would say, and acknowledged in detail the weight of every one, before facing her with what had happened.

It was when he confessed that he finally saw the problem. As he told her, he felt that in her face, her heart and her womb, she had been hurt. He was focusing on the wrong *he* had done. Even in his self-examination, the focus had been on *him*, whereas all that mattered was the way *she* had been hurt. He was gripped by uncontrollable weeping.

But behind all the failures of moralism lies something stronger than steel. It is the willingness to suffer for love, to forgive seventy times seven, and to go the extra mile. It is the attitude which is so committed to the other person that it will go with the problems. This is not cold duty, but is described by Jesus as full of joy and gladness. It is not even the kind of self-satisfaction which comes from being seen by others to suffer. It ploughs on for the good of the other, knowing that God's love is a stronger truth than any obstacle it might encounter. This kind of perseverance outlasts duty; it carries on when duty has become hollow, and most of us begin to glimpse what it means only when we face the life, death and resurrection of Christ.

Chapter 5

LOVE AS HAPPINESS

Since Thomas Jefferson coined the idea that the pursuit of happiness is one of the basic rights of humankind, it has featured strongly in the West. For many people, the great unwritten law of life is that they want to be happy. The key love relationship must therefore be the one that makes them happy. Clichés such as 'They both lived happily ever after' describe the way many of us expect to live. The fairy story is for real. People therefore make checks every day to see whether they are happy or not; it is the thermometer of existence, and the central measure of the success of relationships.

Yet what this great idea means is not always clear. Contentment, enjoyment, pleasure and satisfaction sum up aspects of the central theme. Jeremy Bentham, the English Utilitarian philosopher, developed a more general understanding of happiness. Everybody, he argued, sought pleasure and wanted to avoid pain, whether physical or psychological. They therefore calculated which actions, friendships and relationships gave them the most pleasure, and sought them, or avoided those which on balance had a more negative effect. On this argument, all relationships involve a search for pleasurable rewards, even those which seem to involve altruistic behaviour, because this kind of behaviour too brings psychic pleasure to the subject. Bentham taught that pursuing the greatest happiness of the greatest number was the aim of public policy. Everybody wants to be happy and there is no point to relationships which do not give people pleasure.

Happiness is never having to say you are sorry, wearing his vest and sitting by the fire with one mug of cocoa. It is a commonplace that the business of love is making each other happy. Being happy – 'Smile, please!' – is a requirement on many occasions. Almost all married couples will remember the face-ache which followed the wedding; they were happy, but the effect of one more smile for the photographer, so that posterity would know that this was a glad occasion, was just too much. When finally alone, they gazed at each other with long faces, relaxing the muscles that could take no more. Yet after the wedding, the first requirement was to make the partner happy. They would do anything to make it happen. So the agenda is built up. But what does it actually mean?

'Happiness' is an odd, self-defined, inner state of contentment. It is when I am what I wanted to be. It is the best of all possible worlds for me when all pain, problems, sadness and discomfort are chased away. Each of us has a question to which our happiness is the answer. It is subjective, so each of us can be happy in his or her own way. This allows it to be a live-and-let-live affair. It just depends, as they say, on what turns them on. Sometimes it is model trains, going to the races or staring into the eyes of the beloved. Some of us are never happier than when we are having a good cry. Nobody has to dictate what happiness will be; you just decide it yourself and get on with it. And it is potentially warmhearted; we all wish everybody else a happy Christmas. You wouldn't want them to have a bad time, would you? So love is the commitment to making one's partner happy in this sense of bringing about that inner state of contentment. It should be quite simple.

The culture of happiness

There was a time (some men sigh for it still) when the definition of happiness for a woman was to find the (right) man. The man embodied so many of the woman's life circumstances through his job, attitudes, income and family that she could effectively sink all her dreams in him. This view involved no strongly individualized set of desires, but meant taking up the roles and opportunities which were offered by the newly created family unit.

During this epoch, which in some families has lasted up to the present, ideas of happiness were firmly embedded in social customs which were often associated with family and leisure. Holidays, picnics, parties, family gatherings and sports contained moments of celebration set in well-defined social patterns. Within them, people were glad and sad, but the search for happiness was usually circumscribed by hard work and family commitments.

Only with the fifties in the States and the sixties in Europe did a younger generation have scope to construct their own culture of happiness. It was the era of Harold Macmillan's 'You've never had it so good', Elvis Presley, Cliff Richard's *Summer Holiday*, and a youth culture which aimed to enjoy itself in its own way. Or so it seemed. But records, soft drinks and clothes were sold by adults aiming at profits, and making people happy developed as a highly successful commercial art form. Provided you had the cash, it was within your grasp; you just reached out your hand and plucked the flower. Instant relationships arrived. The hippie culture offered the love-in, the idea that the pleasure of sex should be severed from any need to relate to the partner. If it made you happy, that was fine. Soon this individualistic Utopia was dampened with tears as couples woke up the next morning to relationships which had to mean something or nothing.

But an inner change was taking place in the meaning of love; it was moving towards a subjective state of happiness where every person had private longings, hopes and fantasies which played the tune of love for him or her. Like ancient troubadours, they undertook the long search from town to town, singing the song which they believed would find an echo. Some developed a commitment to the pleasure-principle in sex. They calculated which techniques gave the most sexual pleasure, and sought the Big One, discarding failures as they travelled on. The personal relationships involved scarcely seemed to matter. Another focus was on experience; some shared experiences were pleasurable, and the young hoped that in some relationships enough of these could be strung together to make a permanently pleasurable bundle of subjective rewards.

It was about this time that the assumed identity of happiness between man and woman was thoroughly fragmented. The 'angry young men' of the late fifties (John Osborne, Alan Sillitoe and others) hit out against the domesticating housewife and family, but they merely detonated a far bigger explosion. The early feminists vocalized the possibility that men, rather than making women happy, were often a source of great pain and depression. Women were fed up with spending so much of their lives trying to keep men happy. The concept which had been so full of optimism in the fifties and sixties became much more problematic as the happiness of men and women diverged. Some held on to another version through the materialist dream of being able to buy happiness, but the face of Paul Getty, the richest and the saddest man in the world, denied any link between money and joy. Now the idiom of happiness lives on in the hope of each new generation, but in the adult world it is a disintegrating idol. We can find a bit of it to worship if we want to, but most of us are aware of the emptiness of the happy culture. It is now strung out on artificial smiles, television quiz shows and the Christmas booze-up – part of the sentimental froth of life awaiting the next day's hangover.

Making (her) happy

We need to examine why this trend has occurred by looking at the internal meaning of happiness for relationships. Already, some of the implications of this approach become evident. If the ultimate value is her happiness, everything else has an instrumental role. Slowly, the primacy of her happiness is imposed over different areas of life. He must humour her to keep her happy. She wouldn't be happy with that. Gradually, activities and motives are shaped around maintaining these inner, subjective feelings of well-being, which become more capricious and unpredictable as they are fed with egocentric food. Rather than relationships having value and requiring mutuality, they are seen as feeding this subjective sense of well-being.

This demands that he be a means of making her happy and that he subordinate the significance of all the daily activities of life to this end. Eventually, he feels used by the one who must always be happy, and who sucks in pleasant experiences and satisfaction from those around her. The holiday is just to make her happy; it is not a shared experience. Making love is a question of helping her to enjoy herself and not of mutual expression and receiving. So the self-centredness of the drive leaves partners feeling lonely, either as they live in their own search for happiness and face the depressions which go along with it, or as they try to meet their partner's unslakable thirst for satisfaction.

Yvonne faced the problem of Gordon's overwhelming concern for her happiness at the office. It meant that she was never really able to relate to him properly. She puzzled over the best way of changing things without dishonouring his love.

One of the ways he tried to demonstrate his concern was by constant offers of a drink, and she decided to act there. The next day she accepted every offer and consumed nine cups of tea and coffee. Gordon willingly made each one with a smile and usually had one himself; he showed no irritation, although the offers did tail off slightly in the afternoon. Yvonne's blood turned a watery brown, and her only consolation was that he kept having to go to the toilet. The next day she changed her tactics and offered him drinks. This was unusual, for normally there was no need to do so. At 10:30, when she appeared smiling round the door and offered him his third cup of coffee, he grinned and gave in and their relationship began.

This approach becomes the great engineering project of life. The husband wants the wife to be happy, and becomes a comfort zone for her. He provides a nice home, takes her out, gives her exotic presents, and tries to make her life exciting, and the relationship becomes warped. Although he is doing all this for her, he is not actually being a person she can relate to. He is often so busy worrying over things that he is not there as a person. Sometimes it does not occur to him that his company is what she wants, because he thinks of himself all the time as a restaurant waiter, bringing her what she demands. There is an underlying insecurity, because unless he can make her happy the relationship is doomed. He is anxious, watching her to see if this state (which is the core of the relationship) can be maintained. Anything which might upset her becomes taboo. Gradually, he works out a way of life which conforms to this design, but it is one where he does not participate in a marital relationship, but merely ministers from the outside to her internal state of well-being or misery. Inevitably, because he is ignored, he builds up resentment because issues in his life are not being addressed.

The other partner's lot is no better. She is forced by the focus of the relationship to be concerned with her inner feelings of elation or pain. Moreover, she is led to believe that these have some kind of ultimate significance, and constantly tests them with a subjective thermometer. When it is up, she is up, and when it is down, she is very, very down. She is at the mercy of this subjective state.

Also built into this model is a very powerful pattern of dependence. She is like the child who continually needs to be the centre of attention or to be entertained. When adults are not doing what they should, the child sulks or throws a tantrum. He needs to be kept amused. Similarly, the woman who needs her man to keep her happy is locked into a debilitating dependence. Just as a child may cry or sulk when he has not received a sweet, she walks around with a form of this syndrome; she is upset that life has not made her happy.

He may take on mood manipulation, so that if she feels depressed or unhappy, he develops a series of diversionary tactics which will help her feel better. Gradually, as the moods become more developed, the tactics have to become more extreme; a headache requires a Mediterranean cruise. Yet still the responses fail to address the basic problem, the need to be made happy. Even more seriously, the two are not able to share sorrow and grief in their desire to escape from it into a chin-up mood. Moreover, the weight of this task is depressing for him as he realizes he will never be able to make her happy whatever he does. Faced with his failure, he loses the optimism which has driven him on; his agenda for love cannot work, and he must question either his love or his philosophy.

Janet felt different from last year. They had had a holiday in the Bahamas, and really it had been a good one. Phil had been pleasant as usual, but the wait at Heathrow had spoiled things from the beginning, and the other problem was just how many people there had been around. She longed for empty beaches where there was nobody to intrude on her enjoyment, but there had always been somebody else spoiling the view or making a noise. It seemed you had to pay the earth to have a holiday on some exotic island to be really happy. Phil had been OK, but it hadn't been a very exciting holiday for him either. This year they had no option but to spend less. The holiday brochures full of crowded Spanish beaches sickened her. It was probably the last holiday before they started a family, and the thought of it made her depressed. Whatever holiday they had was bound to be a failure.

The agenda of this motive is bound to fail. It contains an inherent impossibility. When we enjoy something, it is the *thing* which we enjoy; our pleasure results from whatever has caused it. To say that 'we enjoy ourselves' is strictly inaccurate; our 'selves' are precisely what we do not enjoy; indeed, joy is an unself-conscious state which is focused on whatever is its source. Normally, the things to which we respond in this way are those which are good; we may kid ourselves at times that other things are pleasurable, but it is love, beauty, good actions, relationships, the natural world, gentleness, honesty and food which provoke pleasure simply because of what they are. Yet if our central concern is our happiness, the self-centredness of the attitude prevents us from relating to things as they actually are. The possibility of joy is ruled out by the egocentric preoccupation. Thus the man who sees the women around him in terms of the sexual pleasure they might give him cannot simply enjoy their dignity and beauty. Because the happiness motive tries to put the subject at the centre of the universe, it actually cuts him or her off from what can give joy. The quest for happiness makes all the resultant feelings counterfeit.

By contrast, the biblical understanding of blessing is surprising and quite different. Rather than being something which is pursued, blessing has to be given by God, and the terms on which it is given are non-egocentric. Christ made the odd request that people lose their lives and thereby give up the centrality of concern with their own gratification. God gives blessing to those who are not full of themselves, who mourn, who are meek, who deprive themselves to obtain justice for others, who are merciful, peacemakers and pure. In other words, because there is a deep commitment to what is good in God's terms, a person experiences the joy associated with that goodness, even in a context of suffering. Thus it is more blessed to give than to receive, because the focus on what will benefit others allows love to flourish. There is no escape from this law; if our motives really are selfish, they will contaminate what we hope will make us happy, but in so far as our motives and love are pure, we shall experience (although we do not seek) blessing.

Newspaper and slippers

The egocentric reference point of this view makes the other partner expendable. Only as long as she succeeds in keeping him happy is the relationship a stable one, and if all he sees in her is what makes him happy, he is going to have a shallow and unrewarding relationship. Sometimes the demands are nebulous, like the powerful one that says, 'Do not mess up my life with your problems, but keep me blissfully ignorant.' The wife will handle the income tax, schooling, clothing, childcare, family relationships, Christmas cards, holidays, washing and ironing, paying bills and looking after the pets, while he watches snooker and doesn't want to be disturbed. Or perhaps all kinds of problems emerge in the relationship which he will not acknowledge even when they are chronic, because he doesn't want his happy existence to be troubled by anything serious. And they are happily married, aren't they? Eventually, she walks out or bangs her head on the wall, and he is surprised. 'I didn't realize you felt this way,' he says.

At other times his agenda of happiness swamps her daily life. The husband's concern with keeping fit and enjoying exercise means that money and time are spent on his leisure and fitness activities while she is just expected to stay fit through housework. He needs his social contacts – golf, pub, football, office friends – and she baby-minds. The good life for him generates washing, housework and domestic disruption, and she is supposed to sort it out and do a job. He is content and she walks up the wall.

Sadly, there is also a well-trodden route from this kind of indulgence and concern with happiness into extramarital affairs and new relationships. When his concern is whether she will make him happy, it creates a number of possible responses. When he is feeling sorry for himself, he imagines situations and people who might make him more happy. Not surprisingly, given that he has been so self-indulgent at home, he feels guilty there and looks for other, more congenial surroundings. Because the idea of someone making him happy is so flawed to start with, it develops into a quest, moving on from one person to another. Within this context, all kinds of floating relationships occur which have a mutual happiness massage as their chief agenda. They may work for a while in their own terms, but sooner or later the issue of whether his pattern will ever give rise to a real relationship occurs, since the original terms of its development work against it.

There is, of course, another tradition in which women are asked to make men 'happy' on a consumption basis through prostitution and pornography. Here we reach the end of the line, where sex is seen completely in terms of egocentric gratification, and the relationship is reduced to a transaction or a piece of paper. The loneliness of this approach becomes evident. The woman who serves as a prostitute knows that there is no love in the process, but only gratification. She therefore presumably conducts the relationship in those terms, while the man is really only having an extended conversation with himself – what turns him on, what sexual experience he can hang on to for a while, and what it feels like for him. Gratification becomes divorced from care. The magnitude of the problems which grow out of this attitude is demonstrated by Aids, for in the act which, above all, is supposed to express love, it seems that men and women are prepared to pass on death.

Another, more mundane, aspect of this vision is also disturbing. The inner search for happiness has become so deeply part of the consumer culture of our day that people spend large quantities of time surrounding themselves with things, experiences, forms of entertainment, sources of excitement and novelties which they hope will leave them happy and content. This transaction is so routine in daily life that it becomes ritualistic. We pay for a meal or a film and wait for it to make us content or to entertain us. Increasingly, these items create an absorbing environment – watching television, listening to a personal stereo, the exotic holiday or the luxurious home. The subject orders his environment in a way intended to bring him pleasure, as he gets what he wants. In the past, only the rich had servants to wait upon them, but now many more people are into the 'What would you like, sir?' consumer culture and the indulgence which goes with it.

When relationships are seen and structured in similar terms, the damage caused by this perspective become clear. It becomes important for the girlfriend or the wife not to be an inconvenience, and to fit in with the comfortable surroundings. When a direct demand is made, it is irritating and needs to be marginalized. Relationships are programmed like an evening's television viewing; the girl-friend is switched on when it is suitable. The underlying impersonality of this kind of relating is so ordinary that it is easy to ignore it; yet it chokes the roots of a real, loving relationship, strangling it with trivia and self-indulgence.

What is striking about this goal of happiness is the way it creates inner dreams which are basically destructive, because they are tainted by the selfishness and whims of the subject. When these are imposed on the world, what is supposed to be nice, happy and harmless turns out to be evil and to display a fundamental disrespect for others. Because the inner idea is so indulgent, it is often difficult for us to see how damaging and hurtful are its consequences. The idea which many people associate so closely with love is actually an evil selfishness.

The corruption of the search for happiness goes deep. It is a bid to put oneself at the centre of the relationship. It is asking the other person to worship one's own wants. By this central religious act, the sensitivity and oneness of a relationship are warped, and it becomes difficult to receive what the other person has to offer. As in the story of Midas, everything which this motive touches is turned into the uniform gold of what one person wants, and loses its individuality and sparkle. So it is inevitable that the search for happiness will be married to depression and introspective pathos as the underlying cosmic loneliness of the quest becomes apparent.

Making others unhappy

Of course, we feel instinctively that life should be joyful and pleasant. Children often convey an uncomplicated sense of total enjoyment which makes much adult behaviour seem morose, sulky or uptight. Perhaps this is partly because in the adult world many of us spend a lot of time deliberately, or unconsciously, making others unhappy. It is such an obviously spoilsport, dog-in-the-manger attitude that it is often difficult to admit what is happening and why. Yet the argument goes along these lines: 'If *I* am not happy, why should *they* be happy?' And so a number of strategies are developed – a permanent frown, making sure that the others are always under the cloud when it rains, a sense of hurt, or just giving out the message that it is not right under any circumstances to be happy. The source of this attitude may be a legitimate feeling that one's hurts or circumstances are being ignored; but because the idiom of happiness is being manipulated, the outcome is destructive, especially when it becomes a long-term pattern.

Sometimes the source is as simple as the fact that the subject's parents made sure that he or she was not happy as a child, and he or she becomes intent on passing on the same feelings to the next generation. He or she *needs* to look on the dark side and to punish those who are joyful. Whatever the cause, it should be sought out and uprooted before it is imposed on others.

Blessings and joy

Of course, many people *are* happy, or (to use more solid terms) they experience blessings and joy throughout much or part of their lives. In fact, a little joy can go a very long way – through suffering and separation. The Christian understanding of happiness is rigorous; only what is good leads to blessing. And, of course, we are surrounded by good things and wonderful people each day of our lives, even when we are in a prison cell and can only see a square of sky and pray for our family. To thank God for those given to us, and to recognize again how wonderful and beautiful they are, is already to leave the vanity of happiness and link up again with the joys of the real world. There is a difference between the depression and recrimination of happiness-seeking and relationships which are committed to love and care, returning good for evil and putting the other person first. Then joy happens as a by-product in the most normal places – seeing the beauty of those old hands, recognizing the sound of the footsteps on the pathway or looking at the face which you can read down to the last millimetre of muscle movement. And always behind each of these experiences of goodness is the awesome generosity of God, extravagant with blessings and not allowing the second best.

The terms on which we receive blessing are that we be poor in spirit, that we mourn when something really is wrong, and that we be meek, hungry and thirsty to live fairly, always ready to forgive, and out for peace. It is those who suffer for good, who are pure in their motives, who are not self-elated, who enter into the meaning of suffering and who are humble before God who are given the joy of knowing a life lived in tune with God. Because joy is God-given, we must hang on to the God who gives it, not to the joy itself. It is those who truly love God and one another who experience joy. Joy is at God's disposal as a fruit of his Spirit working in our lives. It is not a possession we can claim for ourselves. The big challenge for all of us is therefore whether we work at our own agenda for happiness, or whether we open up our lives to God and to the terms of God's love. Then the richness of those with whom we live becomes evident and blesses us. There is more than a little possibility that God has a better idea of what will really bless us than we have when we dream our own little dreams of happiness.

Chapter 6

LOVE AS SEX

The pleasure principle?

Perhaps the most pervasive idea of love over the last decade or so is that it means sex. When people say 'love', they mean 'going to bed'. The question arises as to whether sexual activity in western societies reflects this point of view. It is not obvious that it does; going to bed with someone may reflect a fear of loneliness or a desire for happiness rather than a belief in sex. It may reflect a desire to show her who is the boss, or to prove how attractive one is. But although it is probably not the only component, the evidence seems to suggest that people believe that sex is the dynamic of love. They believe in sex as the great pleasure principle which will create a relationship of love. It is one of the great commitments of our age. Sex manuals offer to 'improve your love life', with the implication that if things go well in bed, everything else will go well too. The argument goes (in so far as it is consciously expressed) that sex is pleasurable, therefore sex is good, and so it must be a good basis for a relationship of love. If we have pleasure in bed together, we shall love one another.

Yet often something else is conveyed. Earlier periods developed industries which offered sexual pleasure largely dissociated from love. Mayhew estimated that the number of prostitutes in London in 1862 was 80,000.[1] Yet now the public industry is greater. The scale of pornography and prostitution suggests that many people do believe in sex and will pay for their beliefs. The sales of the pornography industry, whose magazines have outsold *Time* or *Newsweek*, are considerable. The outlets rival those for food in many areas. Prostitution, massage parlours, sex shows, adult movie clubs and all kinds of other providers of consumer sex flourish in our cities. The message of these establishments is quite clear: 'We shall give you bodies which will arouse you sexually, and grant you what your body desires.' Although many of the suppliers in this industry are avowedly not sexually motivated, but directed by money, there is little doubt that the vast consumer demand comes from those who want bodies for sexual arousal. Already we see the ambivalence of this focus; on the one hand, sex promises love, and on the other, one can have sexual pleasure without the need for any loving relationship. Thus the argument changes and says: 'Sex is pleasurable and therefore good, and so it should be on offer without any of the encumbrances of love or relationships.'

Given that the sexual-arousal industry is so pervasive, it is likely that both these views deeply influence many of the relationships which take place on a non-commercial basis. At root, being in bed with a woman or man and enjoying it either makes love or substitutes for it. We are therefore addressing not just pornography and prostitution, but an attitude common in many marriages and other love relationships. The argument of this chapter is that this view not only fails as a good basis for love, but also that it is not even good sex.

Much sexual experience is not pleasurable. In a recent study, young women used the following terms to describe having sex: 'It just happened', 'awfully painful', 'cringing', 'quite drunk', 'regretted it', 'crying', 'I felt awful', 'I would rather get up and make a cup of tea.'[2] Many people experience sex as defeat, failure or an empty activity. Indeed, there is abundant evidence that men seek pleasurable sex with women and girls in ways which are predatory and aggressive, and this causes pain on the part of the women. Because the sexual relationship is an egocentric search for pleasure in which the woman is used, her non-participation in the event arouses resentment in the man. What starts out as a quest for pleasure finishes as the opposite, not just for the woman, but also for the man. The terms on which the gratification was sought were, so to speak, self-refuting.

Yet many men can be so addicted to their own self-gratification that it takes them ten or twenty years to work out this simple point, and in the meantime they do much damage to themselves and others.

Rex had been to bed with Ruby four times now. He cast his mind back over the experiences. His earlier sexual relationships had been casual and a bit unsatisfactory, but this was different. She had a nice body, and he felt that sex was better each time. He was elated by the situation, and after a quick drink they went straight back to his place. They settled down and he put his arm round her.

A few minutes later it happened. He shifted the position of his arm and began to say, 'I prefer . . .'

Even as the words came out, he swallowed them. He saw her face harden. Ruby felt that on the basis of his past experiences he was going to suggest what she should do, and she was right. 'I don't want to be just another one,' she said.

Rex didn't want her to be that either, but, because he had been hoping that she would be better than the others, he couldn't handle the situation. She left twenty minutes later with damp eyes and informed him that he would not be seeing her again. He turned and beat the sofa with his fist. When he wandered over to the window, she had already disappeared and it was pouring with rain. She would get very wet.

In summary, when sexual gratification is selfish and egocentric, it involves using the other person in a way which kills the possibility of giving and receiving pleasure. Conversely, when the pleasure of the other person is the focus, giving and receiving pleasure are possible. The question is: when is seeking the pleasure of the other person genuinely what is going on in a sexual relationship? Clearly, it can only be when love is present and an ego-centric search for pleasure is not.

Sexual behaviour and it

One of the chief preoccupations of the last few decades has been with sexual behaviour and its improvement. It has generated a research and counselling industry which has functioned on the idea that if you know how sex works in a biological sense, then you can improve it for humans. The research of Kinsey at first focused on gall wasps. He collected between two and four million of them over a period of twenty years. Later, he brought the same codifying techniques to bear on people's sex histories. He aimed to complete a hundred thousand sex histories, although the Kinsey Report was based on only a few thousand. Nevertheless, the impact of his reports on the sexual behaviour of thousands of men (1948) and women (1953) was to make people aware of sexual behaviour as a category on its own.

The work of Masters and Johnson, which reached the public in the mid-sixties, focused on a detailed examination of the body's response to erotic stimulation. Kinsey concentrated on reports, Masters and Johnson on direct clinical experiments. The emphasis of their book *Human Sexual Response* (1966) was on the physiological changes which take place during coitus and orgasm. Their 1970 study examined the psychological aspects of sexuality, especially frigidity, impotence and premature ejaculation. Such studies helped some couples who faced problems in their sexual lives which they could not overcome, but their main theme was sexual performance. The wider public perception of these studies, sex manuals and much related literature was that the male–female problem was one of sexual physiology, which was to be met principally by behavioural and other responses. Recent falls in the birth rate have been put down to the time couples spend in bed reading sex manuals.

It has become evident that the most effective kinds of therapy often involved deconstructing the couple's anxiety about 'it' (*i.e.* having sex), and allowing mutual help and understanding to develop. These therapies were relational and gave love its due place. Thus Kaplan writes, 'Love is the most important ingredient in lovemaking. Making love with someone whom one loves is simply not comparable to such an experience, no matter how technically proficient, sensuously free and even gentle, with an unloved partner.'[3] Yet, sadly, this was not the central thrust of the sex industry; it conveyed the message that sexual physiological satisfaction was love. We should be quite clear that this message is largely driven by money-making, not by a search for the truth.

There was actually something quite manipulative going on in all this. On the one hand, gall wasps, rabbits and most of the rest of the creation did it to good effect without sex manuals and counsellors. And the human species seems to have got on with reproduction fairly well over the last few millennia. So the aim of sex was not merely effective copulation. The real focus of all these studies was on what sex meant to people, on its psychic dynamics, and here their assumptions were evident. If couples achieved a suitable level of mutual sexual arousal, if the performance was good, then sex was a success. Masters and Johnson and others were clear that marital commitment or love was not on the agenda, but merely the immediate performance of the act. Thus bodily contact matters more than the person with whom it is achieved. Sex was to be dissociated from friendship, trust, commitment and having fun in the rest of life. It is actually a deconstruction of intimacy; what is potentially part of an intimate, shared relationship becomes an instant turn-on. The use of couples in an experimental situation, observing their performance with a relative disregard for their long-term relationship, showed that this was the emphasis in the Masters and Johnson studies. The framework of analysis was essentially a stimulus-response model used in many physiological studies with animals.

This attitude is not confined to laboratories. The concern with sex as performance was pushed as a new campus industry. Sex manuals encouraged it. Many men were worried about their virility, and the fear of impotence is probably more widespread now than it has ever been. There was an industry of sexual stimuli which presumably implied that being together was no longer good enough. There is a problem with this whole approach. The stimulus-response model contains its own weaknesses. Will the stimulus be enough next time? What will he need to turn him on? How well do I need to perform? Like the progression from soft to hard pornography in the search for ever greater stimuli, this search for sexual performance is restless and has no peaceful answer. Because at root it holds the other person as of little account, except as a performing body, it becomes an impersonal routine concerned about having 'it', and is devoid of interpersonal chemistry.

Tom had made love to Pamela a dozen or so times in their three-month friendship. This time a problem surfaced which had lain half buried for a few weeks. Tom wasn't sure what to think about during the act. He knew his thoughts had to be sexual if he were to get the most out of it. He could dwell on breasts and bottoms, but there was only so much to think about and his mind strayed to other things. He tried to concentrate on the performance and on doing well, but the more he did that, the more difficult it seemed to become. He could fantasize, but that didn't seem to be right by Pam. As he glanced at her face, he saw that she wasn't really concentrating either, and he asked her what she was thinking.

'Actually, I'm wondering whether it's going to rain with the washing out.'

Tom shrank and felt very annoyed. They lay back, and then it did start to rain. Pam dressed quickly, rushed out and came back with a damp pile of washing which she dumped on the table and folded. When she came back to bed, Tom tried to think about sex, but however hard he thought, nothing happened. Pam got out of bed and started the ironing.

The problem of the sexual focus is very common. A well-documented female feeling is summed up by the phrase, 'All he seems to want is sex.' The woman (usually) becomes aware that her partner shows relatively little interest in her – her feelings, interests, concerns and worries – but becomes interested when the possibility of going to bed arises. She thinks (and perhaps says), 'You don't really want me; you just want my body.'

He may protest, but the intimate relationships which follow are clouded by a lack of commitment on the part of the woman, which reflects the resentment she feels at being treated as no more than an object of the man's sexual pleasure. This attitude is so widespread that it is institutionalized. A few decades ago it was understood that when a girl became pregnant, she had caught the man. He, it was assumed, was interested only in sex, but when a baby came he had to accept the full package whether he liked it or not. At a guess, resentment at being sexually used must have a far more dampening effect on the sexual life of the West than all the titillation of pornography and sexual stimuli. All over the West, people are having worse sexual relations because the emphasis on impersonal sex leaves them (women especially, but also increasingly men) feeling used and depersonalized.

Much of this pattern reflects the commercial exploitation of sex. There are men and women in executive houses, becoming part of the local establishment, who have made a lot of money out of selling pornography, prostitution and other forms of consumer sex. They are presumably more interested in money than in sex, and their technique is to offer a commercial 'product', which is, as they would say, 'harmless'.

This idea is mythical. Sex is used to exploit people. Pornographic magazines are not likely to be as cheap as, say, *Motorcycle Weekly*, because they prey upon personal weaknesses. It is so taken for granted that the sex consumer will be ripped off that nobody questions why the margins of profit are not the same as at the local corner shop. Obviously, the women and children involved are exploited and intimidated. This represents the success of a destructive process encouraged by some tabloid newspapers and other publications which use sex to produce sales. People are enticed into sexual experience, fantasy, voyeurism and lust through commercial methods which are similar to those used in selling soap powders. The hope is always for something 'better', but the search which this industry promotes always leads to something worse. The lie on which the whole industry feeds is that sex is a consumer good, an 'it'. As with other addictive industries, people need help to cut the addiction; its false claims must be exposed and its peddlers prosecuted. What they deal in is not so much filth as unloved bodies.

The dissociation of sex, as an 'it', from the rest of life is bound to be a problem. It destroys personal integrity and wholeness. It makes people feel distant from or trapped by their bodies. Sex often becomes strangely emotionless, an activity which is indeed like sleep. It occurs outside normal life and depends on fantasies. Thus, not surprisingly, many experience sexual activity as compromising their personal integrity and even as something destructive for them. They are, in some way or another, at war with 'it'. At root, the problem arises from seeing it as an 'it' in the first place.

The integrity of our bodies

A Christian understanding of bodies recognizes that we *are* our bodies. God has created us, first as babies and then as adults, as bodies. We are wonderfully made, down to the way in which our blood corpuscles fold up in order to pass through our capillaries. We are not 'in' our bodies; Jesus rose bodily from the garden tomb and ate a fish to show his disciples he was alive. Nor are we merely bodies in a physiological or reductionalist sense, for, just as the creation is a mixture of what is seen and unseen, so are we. In recognition of this truth, the Bible does not compartmentalize personhood into mind, body, spirit and soul, but uses the terms interchangably. Thus Paul, in telling us what our response to God should be like, says this:

> 'Offer your bodies as living sacrifices, holy and pleasing to God – this is your spiritual act of worship. Do not conform any longer to the pattern of this world, but be transformed by the renewing of your mind. Then you will be able to test and approve what God's will is – his good, pleasing and perfect will' (Romans 12:1–2).

This and many other biblical statements affirm the integrity of our bodies before God; they are temples of God's Spirit. They have been created 'very good', and we are to be at one with them.

Sin and evil destroy this integrity in a number of serious ways. Poverty and famine weaken and destroy many bodies. Social judgment of the fat, thin, short and tall damages the bodily identity of many. The distortion of appetite by greed, dieting, drugs and addiction leaves many people at perpetual war with their bodies. Because of past sexual experiences involving abuse or sexual hypocrisy, some do not feel honoured or honourable in their bodily existence. Throughout the history of peasant and industrial labour, bodies have been abused by the work demanded of them. In North America and Europe, these abuses have been largely tackled; but in their place have come other forms of physical and mental stress which are more insidious, associated with travel, pollution, noise, the media and sleeplessness. And, as our biblical perspective would lead us to expect, many bodily problems are psychosomatic, growing out of personal problems which remain unresolved. But strangely, although these problems are serious, in the West the primary problem for the body comes from the worship of it.

The dominant form is worship of the female body by men. This worship is not real, but involves collusion between male fantasies, demands and hopes on the one hand, and, on the other, the willingness of women to conform to and sustain myths. Men who want sex as a physiological experience create a demand for and encourage stereotypical female bodies which meet their wishes and fantasies. The history of this pattern includes Chinese foot-binding, bustles, and, today, models, pin-ups and sex objects. Freedman has made the point that beauty is imprisoned as women strive for the physical perfection demanded by men, and in the process live confined lives, pressured by fashion, cosmetics, diets, notions of attractiveness and the need to appeal.[4] Trying to be an idol is hard work. Because the stereotype is young and characterless, it dishonours the real beauty of women. Now, of course, a similar idiom of male-body worship is growing to make the pattern more nearly symmetrical. Both forms miss the real point of the given, created beauty of men and women. When travelling on the London Underground, I as a portrait painter experience the awesome beauty of face after face in the carriage. But perhaps the deepest beauty of all occurs when hearts and bodies reflect the love of God and of one another. Then beauty is no longer bound, but free and easy.

The worship of nature

Something even deeper is going on in this worship of the body. It is part of a culture which locates the body not in God's good creation and our personhood, but in nature. This paganism identifies the body as one with nature, Mother Earth, the life force and the primal forces which shape human destiny. Within this perspective, rather than being the expression of marital love, sex is a religious act of identification with the life force. It is the great religious mystery of life which puts its advocates in touch with the source of their being. The ancient nature religions, with their Ashtaroths, high places, Dionysian cults and so on, tended to feature orgiastic rites because sexual consummation was central to their creation myths and was the act in which identification with nature's deities was most complete. Thus sex was a rite of impersonal worship, a way of finding one's identity through the great natural act, not a statement of love. Throughout history the worship of nature has tended to be accompanied by sex as worship. This is what Paul describes in Romans 1, and his argument about Greek and Roman culture is crucial. He writes:

> Although [people] knew God, they neither glorified him as God nor gave thanks to him, but their thinking became futile and their foolish hearts were darkened. Although they claimed to be wise, they became fools and exchanged the glory of the immortal God for images made to look like mortal man and birds and animals and reptiles. Therefore God gave them over in the

sinful desires of their hearts to sexual impurity for
the degrading of their bodies with one another.
They exchanged the truth of God for a lie, and
worshipped and served created things rather than
the Creator (verses 21–25).

This nature worship and its reflection in seeing sex as the
key to human identity have re-emerged in the culture of
the modern West.

It has often developed in the context of a mind–body
split. The body represented a blind force which was dark
and dangerous. Within this way of thinking, nature
worship was frequently identified with women, with the
power of women and with witchcraft. It therefore needed
to be controlled by the mind, which was seen as keeping the
body in subjection. Whenever the body seemed likely to get
out of control, the mind should step in and steady things
down a bit. The body was concerned with sex, and the
mind with love – Platonic love, duty, purity and proper
marital and family life. These two worlds co-existed in
English Victorian society where the prostitutes on the
streets of London lived alongside table legs which were
kept covered for the sake of modesty.

At the end of the nineteenth century there arose a new
search for the 'natural'. It is found in Gauguin's quest for
the natural life in Tahiti, the rediscovery of savage art, and
the sexual attitudes of Havelock Ellis and other late Victorians. Perhaps the key figures in this development are
Sigmund Freud and D. H. Lawrence. Freud's thought was
complex, but it involved discovering the roots of personal
development in infant sexuality; the body's natural activities became the point of reference for self-understanding,
and the subconscious and dream worlds were seen as
opportunities for connection with the natural self. Naturalistic educators revolted against mind-training by adults,
and naturalism as a nudist movement with an emphasis on
health had a significant impact. In the days when Mediterranean holidays were expensive, thousands of goose-
pimpled bodies at resorts on the south coast of England

extolled the virtues of unclothed living. The motivation for this development was not so much the ideas of Freud and the post-Freudians as the assumption that the truth about ourselves and our relationships was to be found in the natural. William McDougall and others emphasized drives and urges, and social Darwinism similarly conveyed that what is most basic about ourselves is the animal. Much Nazi philosophy and propaganda reflected this view of things. The Arians were the natural people uncorrupted by Jewish intellect or Christian asceticism. Thus the way was opened for many of the old pagan and Dionysian religious themes to re-enter western life.

A similar development can be traced in Lawrence. Early in his life Lawrence was influenced by Christian teaching and used its imagery, but his search for 'god' was carried out on his own terms. His concern was to penetrate to the truth of human existence and relationships free from the destructive encumbrances of culture and the mind. His search for this kind of purity was not promiscuous, but aimed at a rediscovery of healthy life and relationships. But the meaning of life seemed to him to lie more and more in the primal life-force gods of Mexico and elsewhere. He too embarked on a pagan quest which would make sex into the central sacrament of human existence and which he hoped would free people from the corruptions of mind, control and domination.[5] This quest has since been followed by millions who have taken the same cultural road. They have been told that the discovery of their bodies is the key to self-realization and that sex is a religious sacrament which imparts this central truth. Popular culture has conveyed this in different ways. The sex idols of the screen – Monroe, Bardot and their successors – created an initial worship of this idiom, fostered by the media. As a late development of the theme, Madonna poses as a quasi-religious figure and adopts sexual uniforms which reflect this cultic worship.

The underlying motif in this trend is that sex is an act of nature-worship in which the participant experiences the ultimate reality of the wider universe and also of his or her own nature. It is both self-discovery and the discovery of the other. What people actually discover, however, is impersonal, the inner force, 'it', something which has no personal referent or meaning and which merely aligns the participants with the grunts of animals. Sometimes it is contact with the great primal force. Sometimes it is the meeting of yin and yang, the basic male and female principles of the universe. Sometimes it is being in touch at the deepest level with male or female power, so that the phallus or the female body becomes a central image of the universe. All these religious experiences and statements flow beyond the relationship to the basic forces of nature. Of course, this is all rather high-flown and rarified for most people. But popular culture is essentially saying the same thing.

Magazines imply that people find themselves through sex. Everything has to be natural, and new mystical forces are discovered which unlock the natural in all of us. Body cults which idolize the male and female form, often in quite grotesque forms, sell magazines and collect followers. Homosexuality is understood by many to be a natural condition which requires people to 'come out' and identify themselves as 'gay' or lesbian, rather than the outcome of relationships and sexual experience which can be reversed. Fetishes of male and female power lead to peculiar sexual practices, and some groups indulge in dangerous forms of ritual sex. Throughout, a continual refrain chants that sex is natural, therefore it is good. It is part of human nature, and even the point at which we are most fully ourselves, because we are at one with the nature gods and goddesses of the universe.

The effects of this view are devastating. The meaning of sex has nothing to do with the unique relationships of the persons who are involved in the acts. They are seen to be relating religiously to nature and to their own natural urges in a form of cultic worship. What is called 'love' has its meaning in the physiological acts of mutual bodily stimulation. It is an impersonal act of worship which expresses a pagan belief in the mystery of life. It has often been, and may now be, associated with human sacrifice. Of ultimate religious significance, it cannot be viewed critically or seen as encouraging evil. On this view, rape is OK; it is the same act, with a sacrificial victim. Although there are all kinds of contributory factors in rape, historically and currently this crude, naturalistic philosophy seems to be one of the most serious. A behavioural understanding is based on the idea that a stimulus must evoke a response. This builds in a demand for ever stronger stimulii of the kind seen in hard porn and the more bizarre forms of prostitution. The logic generates the increasingly frenzied abuse of women and children, and sexual rites which are sub-human in the demands they make of the participants. The liberal hope of dispelling fear and ignorance in sexual activity, praiseworthy in its own way, is now swallowed up in this much deeper religion of nature.

It would be easy to focus on the sensational and the unpleasant. But more important, because of its pervasiveness, is the widespread experience of those who seek naturalistic sex and find themselves left with empty relationships. For if the physical act is supposed to be meaningful in itself, then the relationship is incidental. Copulating couples find themselves lonely in their perception that all they are doing is meeting a natural urge. Fulfilling one's nature turns out to be very different from loving one's partner, especially when that nature is selfish, arrogant and self-indulgent.

Sex and truth

The root problem with this view of sex as self-fulfilment is the way it makes sex more basic and fundamental than love. It can be highlighted by looking at various meanings of the sex act.

First, it can be a way of saying with one's body, 'I love you and give myself to you unconditionally, openly and with nothing withheld.' The body-statement 'I love you' is true, and celebrates what is happening in the rest of the couple's life. It grows out of the love and care which they have for each other, and is thus stable because it is truly based. The very intimacy of the relationship opens the question whether the heart of each is pure and given without reservation to the other. The act also means permanent commitment and takes place in a context of unconditional trust. The word 'troth' summarizes a relationship in which the truth of love and self-giving is unconditional, and in which sexual enjoyment follows from it. Without trust of this kind, intimate sexual enjoyment gives way to fear and emotional distance.

Alternatively, it is possible to say with one's body, 'I love you,' without fully meaning it. One may mean, 'I love you, until somebody else comes along,' or 'I love you, but not enough to live with you for life,' or 'I want you to think I love you,' or 'My feeling for you now is very intense, but I may soon get over it.' These statements introduce a lie into the relationship. What the body is saying the heart does not mean.

This leads to two problems. First, one is involved in a form of hypocrisy which is within one's own body; one is physically living a contradiction. One either becomes resigned to living the hypocrisy, or faces its problems. Secondly, the person who is being lied to will sooner or later discover it. Because the relationship is so intimate, the meaning of what is happening will show clearly through the false sexual statement, and the person who has been deceived will be hurt. Millions of people are locked into the hypocrisy and self-deception of their protests of love in bed. They know and regret that their love is cheap. Millions more have been hurt because they have given everything to their partners and learned later that they have been discarded.

To avoid this possibility, many are now opting for a meaning of sex which says that it is just a natural act or a source of satisfaction which has no relationship implications. Although a couple might go to bed together, this is merely mutual gratification and has nothing to do with love. This view actually makes the sex act, which should be intimate and loving, lonely and self-indulgent. It involves turning away from real, loving relationships, and living in a world of subjective gratification. Persons are treated as bodies. There is no need to talk, only to touch flesh.

Biblical truth does not allow anything other than honesty of thought, emotions and body. Our bodies are meant to speak sexual truth in the full context of our relationship with God, with each other and with ourselves. Then the meaning of sexuality becomes far richer, incorporating all we are as men and women. We love and honour our own bodies and those of other people. They are 'very good'. There is no difference for single and married people. Each knows bodily integrity and relates chastely to others, either in faithful marriage or in friendship. Then, too, the truth, or troth, of our relationships is reflected fully in all our bodily relationships. The way we kiss our father, hug our friend, link arms with our neighbour or play tennis with our partner involves true, loving relationships with them all. The destructive possibilities of sin are present in all of them, but so is the goodness of all that God has given us in one another and in our bodies. On the one hand our bodies can lie, kill and destroy, but on the other they can love, work and be temples of God's Holy Spirit in bed and in the rest of life. The truth always finds us out, but the better way is to walk in it.

Chapter 7

LOVE AS COMPATIBILITY

Each of the meanings of love we have considered thus far has its own history in national cultures, families and the lives of individuals. Many of them run concurrently, and one of the pitfalls we must avoid is that of simplifying what is a very subtle picture. Yet there are historical developments in the history of love which, although imprecise, are important, because they reshape the attitudes of many people and relationships. Perhaps the deepest change in the last few decades has been a growth of unbelief in the older humanist views of love – love as romance, feeling, duty, ideal and happiness. A generation of children in North America and Europe has now experienced a quarter to a third of their parents' marriages ending in divorce. They and many other younger people have found that 'love', whatever that means, often does not work. They are, in an obvious sense, the post-romantic generation; they are not going to accept an optimistic model of love and run with it.

Another bit of the picture is the way the older generation has interpreted the failure of these relationships to the younger. By far the most common interpretation has been that Mum and Dad were just not the kind of people who could get on well with one another. They were not compatible, and this became evident as the relationship developed. This, of course, is a useful explanation. It avoids passing judgment on anybody. It opens the way to other relationships which might be successful. Ending the relationship also supposedly solves the problem, for each person can define the other as the one who is not compatible.

Although this is a useful explanation, the question is whether it is true. It may merely be an excuse for fairly frequent changes of relationship, all of which can be declared 'not a good match'. Is a 'love relationship' simply a matter of getting together two people who are a good fit with each other?

The idea of personal compatibility is interesting. Does it mean that prospective partners need to have certain characteristics in common? Or can 'compatible' be dissimilar? If somebody is impatient, it is difficult to know whether he or she is better matched by somebody who is patient or similarly impatient – or perhaps the first person should not be impatient in the first place. Maybe the emphasis should be on what people do – on their lifestyle – rather than on what they are like. On that basis, golfers, churchgoers or compulsive shoppers should marry their fellow players, worshippers and consumers, and have their free-time activities in common. This model almost becomes a question of comparing personal organizers. Yet it is not to be so easily dismissed, because a complex process of sifting does go on among prospective partners, by which they decide whether they want to link up with each other. What is going on in this process, and is the idea of compatibility really basic to man–woman relationships?

Personality types

Dating agencies and computer dating are part of modern relationship-forming. Many of these involve the kind of social sifting which, in past eras, was done by parents, fraternities and sororities or the Young Conservatives. Advertisements in India still reflect these patterns. Prospective partners are expected to detail their education, colour, height, appearance and a list of other qualifications to be vetted by families engaged in a social-placing operation. In the West, a more individualistic idiom operates. People list those characteristics which they think will be liked by the other person. Some computer dating agencies have models of compatibility which are more than just social classification; they involve assumptions about complementarity, similarity or polar attraction. Questionnaires are often used to establish what personalities are like, on the basis of which classifications are made. But the underlying conception is of personalities who fit.

Many of these processes, of course, claim to be more rigorous than they actually are. The success of the dating agencies has much to do with the anonymity of modern city life and the need to have some conventional process, with recognizable stages, whereby people can meet. Yet behind them lies an interesting question. Do people's personalities have fixed characteristics, or are they more plastic and open, able to adapt and change in relationship?

One of the big ideas of humanism is that of the self-made person. Character and personality are built from the inside out. Our culture continually creates personalities; it is the assumed mode of personal growth. These processes often involve publicity, self-projection, image-building and the development of personal style. And when people talk about one another, it is often in the language of personality. 'He is highly strung, quiet and nervous, while she is easy-going, talkative and has no ambition at all; I don't see how they could get on together.' When we are told what kind of personality we have, it is often either to praise or to blame us.

So the idea of personalities is inculcated in many of us. And when the question, 'Why should anyone love me?' is asked, it is assumed that the answer must lie in personality. To be loved, he must be the right type. To remain beloved, she must continue to inhabit the personality which drew him to her. The process of personality development becomes the route to being loved. It might involve education, or appearance, or a certain kind of appeal, but it boils down to being made into the kind of person who can be loved. This idea is tyrannical, both in terms of what individuals believe they have to do to themselves, and also in its impact on others. The model especially destroys the ability of those involved to develop sensitivity in relation to each other.

This is related to the struggle, experienced by many, to

know if they are marrying the right person. Of course, the decision to share one's whole being and life with another person is enormous. Often, we are attracted to people who are like us, which may be a good or a bad thing. But if the decision hinges only on the idea that one person will be right and another wrong simply because of their personalities, it misses a bigger point. It is almost like the artist who believes that the quality of his painting depends on the kind of brush he buys. The fact that a relationship is open, giving, respectful, kind and marked by mutual joy and care indicates not that two personalities fit, but that two persons love one another.

Some personalities are too rigid to adapt fully to a union. Sometimes, weaknesses have to be carried by the other partner for decades. In some partnerships, lack of respect strangles important parts of their lives. People sometimes close down the possibility of growing together. Marriage may compromise a life direction which is part of someone's faith, or it may help it. The delicate and free decision to become married or not must go deeper than personalities; it is more mysterious than that, because it involves all of our personhood, including our faith. Centrally, it concerns whether each person loves the other unconditionally and will give and receive love on God's terms.

Perhaps this issue is made more acute by the modern tendency to get married later in life. People who marry young grow older together, melding and co-operating. Those who meet when they are older have more fully developed 'personalities', and therefore need great sensitivity to each other as they embark on this process. If they have settled into a rigidity which cannot be overcome by love, there are problems. When the richness of earlier experience (including defeats and failures) is fully welcomed into the relationship, most of the awkward corners in people's lives can be rounded. Because the idea of personality is so individualized, however, it discourages the sharing and communication which can make us more open and accessible.

The concept of 'personality types' probably does more

harm than good. Many of us operate with set views of people, even of those we know quite well. We may say they are extravert, sociable, shy, disorganized, intuitive, domineering, emotional or artistic. But to say that they *are* these characteristics creates a too-rigid pattern. All of us, for example, have the experience of seeing a friend behave with somebody else in a way which is quite different from the way he or she would relate to us. Clearly, each relationship has its own unique characteristics which mean that none of us can definitively type-cast another. This type-casting is often simply a result of the treatment being meted out by the person who does the labelling. The boring person merely reflects the lack of interest and respect which the labeller exhibits towards him or her. Each of us is inexhaustibly rich. Those who label others as boring betray their own dismissive attitude that says, 'Won't you make my life exciting?'

People also reflect the way they have been treated by others earlier in life. Many experience a process of growing free from oppressive family backgrounds; they become something different from what they were. This points to the fact that most of us also have some sense of *why* we are such-and-such a type. Perhaps a 'reserved' person has good reasons for not sharing his emotions or thoughts with others; he has been let down, he does not have the words, or he never spoke up at school. When we understand this, we immediately see that there is far more to a person than is conveyed by any of the labels we might apply. Personality-labelling, therefore, is often a dismissive and destructive process.

Monica pushed Tony to be more assertive. She wanted him to be more in control at work and at home. One Friday evening, he came home and announced that he had been appointed national product development manager, a massive promotion. Monica was sensible enough to see that it was not her pushing which had produced this result, and was intrigued to know what was going on. After coffee, she asked him, noting that for once he did not have to defend himself against her pressure.

His answer was interesting. There were a lot of people at work who pushed their products and their way of seeing things. He had been committed to a different line, evaluating products carefully and assessing their limitations. For example, he had recommended against tooling up for a product he himself had been working on. Soon afterwards, other companies in the same product area had lost millions because of market conditions. The directors had noticed, and trusted Tony because he was not assertive.

Tony looked up at Monica. 'Why do *you* need me to be assertive?' he asked.

'I suppose it's because I'm frightened of always getting my own way,' she replied.

'But we won't solve your problem by pretending it's mine,' Tony responded. 'And it isn't as much of a problem for me as you seem to feel it is.'

Although people differ in rich and various ways, Christianity emphasizes an even more open view of personhood. Faith is the direction of life which people take before God and in relation to one another. Faith in God opens us to the ways and purposes of God; it involves becoming as well as being. We ask God to guide and shape our relationships for the better. This can shake us free from rigidities and faults which mar our character and relationships. It is not normally given attributes which create tensions. People seldom remark bitterly that 'he is 5ft 6in tall and has red hair'; bitter comments usually point to bad temper, arrogance, an inability to listen, and laziness. Conversely, misdirected faith can involve growing into harmful, destructive patterns of evil and self-deception. Seen in this perspective, personality can become a problem when individuals tie themselves down into their personae, continuing in whatever wrong attitudes they might have, and losing the sense of the onward development of life before God. The idea of personality becomes nostalgic, and develops rigidities which limit the openness of relationships. Our development of personality also tends to be less rich than the challenges with which each stage of life presents us. In the end, all that matters is the life that each of us lives before God, whose understanding of each of us stretches way beyond any feeble projection of personality.

Lifestyle compatibility

Another variant of this model focuses less on personality and more on lifestyle. It is not very ambitious. In the late twentieth century, many young people see life in terms of organizing a lifestyle. They are in the business of getting their act together, putting together a package, getting it organized. Career, leisure, pleasure, travel, and friends are coordinated in a way which is acceptable and suits them. If the package doesn't work, then it is reprocessed. A characteristic of this approach is the independence with which the participants expect and demand to live their life their way. There are obvious constraints, but these can be negotiated and often pushed back until we get what we want. Traditionally, married women have been asked to fit in with the lifestyles of their husbands; they have adopted the role of servicing their husbands' needs. He had activities, such as golf, football and drinking, which she was expected to support. (I remember meeting one couple whose annual holiday was always organized around attending a Test match. The wife, who at first had no interest in cricket at all, also became addicted to the game, though she really had no option.)

More recently, women have thankfully developed less subservient responses, and along with this has come greater independence of lifestyle. In some relationships, the male–female styles of living diverge, and the question arises how two independent lifestyles can co-exist in a marriage in a viable way. The advice often given is that people should choose partners who fit, who have compatible Filofaxes. On this view, love in its romantic and other varieties is really over the top. There is no point in going overboard when what matters is how the agendas work out. The question then is: what kind of relationship is compatible with my lifestyle?

A common answer to this question is given in terms of activities. If someone can be found who likes the same things and has similar attitudes, then a relationship can be established which will not impose on life, but will enrich it. The terms of the relationship can be negotiated. They can involve sleeping together, but not sharing income. They can involve sex, but not exclusive sex. They can be tried out for a couple of years, after which there will be a review. The approach is cool, and avoids the acute emotional stress and tangled, insoluble problems which occur when two people irrevocably get hitched.

In principle, however, the model also makes for inner reserve and emotional withdrawal. There is no basis for long-term trust of this man or woman, and each makes sure he or she will not get hurt. When a couple feel they do not like each other as much as they did, they drift into a more distant style of living, or even live apart. Actually, this distance can be maintained only at a cost. The way of relating that asserts, 'It doesn't matter to me' is based upon a hardening of the heart and withdrawal through hurt. We can make ourselves insensitive, but the costs are very great, even if we are not aware of them.

Sometimes, this attitude reflects a view of *time* which centres on the idea of getting the most out of life. Behind it are all kinds of calculations which express an attempt to own time. 'My time is my own and I don't want anybody else meddling with it.' Especially, we do not want anybody laying claim to our future, or believing that they have a permanent claim on our lives. This seems harmless enough, but has serious consequences. The New Wet Male is part of this phenomenon. He is characteristically described as incapable of real commitment. He is quite prepared to use a woman while she is young and attractive, but when there is the question of children or of a commitment which would cost him something, he runs back into his independence. Within this way of seeing things, children can be a threat rather than a blessing. Young couples with this approach face the possibility of children as a great trauma, because the care of babies requires that the parents fit into their routines of feeding, sleeping, playing and cuddles. Unless the parents escape from this view, they define the relationship in terms akin to warfare. 'How dare this kid try to mess up my life!' Until both parents (especially the father) let go of their central concern with lifestyle, they cannot bring up children properly.

Human beings, however, do not have dominion over time, nor can they control what happens in it. Our own agenda is frequently so powerful that it tries to dictate what course history should take. But things do not work out that way. We are given each moment by God, and cannot own even one minute for ourselves. Even the smallest, wistful hope of repeating yesterday is pathetic. Time is given by God in all its richness, and only when our past, present and future are entrusted to God do we know eternal life. And part of the joy of life is to love others whose time is just as precious as our own.

Cohabitation

We can now see something of the real meaning of cohabitation. When people cohabit rather than marry, all kinds of things may be happening. Some prefer it to legal marriage because they do not want their relationship to depend on a legal document. This is healthy in so far as it recognizes that commitment is more than a piece of paper, and to that extent it parallels the biblical idea of 'troth', by which a couple bind themselves to live in faithfulness to each other. The decision may just reflect a distrust of legalism and possibly a cold parental marriage. Others are thinking for the present and have not developed a deeper view of the meaning of time in relationships.

But many cohabit in the sense of putting two lifestyles together while retaining a commitment to their own individual ways of life. Sex, for example, may be something which is pleasant and congenial but which implies nothing more – a bit like taking a shower. Almost inevitably, the point occurs in the relationship where the question arises: 'Do you mean more to me than having a shower?' If the answer is 'No', the relationship begins to unravel. Cohabitation thus either tends to grow into something more meaningful (despite its muddled and misguided starting-point) or it reveals the lack of commitment, love, joy and excitement on which it is based. Such a relationship is not two people shaping up to share each other's lives, but a few pages in the Filofax of life.

Keith moved in with Trudy. He enjoyed the change, and it was pleasant being together and doing things outside the busy demands of work. She was younger than he was, attractive and great fun. Sharing costs of the flat was more economical for both of them, and they enjoyed life in bed and out of it.

He noticed a number of erratic patterns of behaviour, but the first time it really struck him (he winced slightly at the thought) was when she threw a glass of water in his face. He would have understood if she had been angry of if something had upset her, but it was in the middle of a pleasant meal. The incidents got worse, but she always refused to comment on them in any way. She said, 'That would be compromise.'

When she got to the stage of pouring a bowl full of cold washing-up water over him in bed, he decided it was time to get out. He concluded afterwards that it was probably safer to have his own place. He wondered why she always seemed to have a fixation on water, and was glad he hadn't got more deeply involved.

The problems with compatibility

The idea of compatibility is thus more disastrous than it seems. There is a hardness in it which demands that she be compatible with him or he with her. Indeed, it is possible to construct compatibility requirements which rule out the whole population as unsuitable. Many people argue themselves into a corner with their exclusive demands as to what their partner should be like, blaming them when they fall short. Quite a few relationships seem to hang on whether it is he or she who decides how a room is decorated. Yet this is preposterous. In practice the strangest people marry each other and get on well despite glaring differences. Although the idea of incompatibility is often used to describe personality differences which make a relationship 'impossible', it usually describes attitudes which prevent sharing, openness and self-sacrifice. Many of us make deep-seated demands regarding the terms on which relating to us is possible. More accurately, they actually define the limits of our love. Real compatibility grows through trust, communication, patience, care, sensitivity and the straightforward biblical principle of putting the other person first. When two people are bonded together in troth, they share their time and commitments; but if the underlying commitment is to their own agendas, then incompatibilities will occur.

Similarly, the idea of attractive or likable personalities proves shallow. He may be a very nice man, but the question is 'Why?' Personality construction is very complex, but, if the focus is on oneself, rigidities occur which are abrasive and insensitive. Over time, real love relationships move beyond even multiple characteristics into more central motives, attitudes and ways of thinking. By contrast, the confusion and complexities which arise from people's personalities actually get in the way of straightforward, open relationships.

The biblical route out of this impasse is found in the radical critique of egocentricity. We are to count others more important than ourselves as a way of redressing our tendency to put ourselves at the centre of the universe. Real humility puts our own wants and desires in the context of what, in God's purposes, is good for all. 'Thy will, not mine, be done' is central to a thorough redefinition of lifestyle and character which recognizes how deep are the respect, cooperation and sharing we need to develop. The meek are compatible; they are the ones who quietly fit in and make cooperation work. In our egoistic culture they tend to go unnoticed, but they are often around.

Nor is there any hope for relationships which are structured only on convenience and suitable lifestyles. Treating one another like fast-food restaurants does not work either. It cheapens, hurts and hardens. The business of living with and relating to a partner over any period of time evokes and demands bonds of love. Many cohabiting relationships collapse into marital love which has real guts to it, but the damage done by the attempt to pretend that intimate personal relationships can be handled like a visit to a hotel is enormous. For, if people are wedded to their lifestyle and treat their partners as a pleasant component of it, the shallowness of the relationship will soon become evident. The central message of Christianity is the steadfast commitment of God to humans who are callous and evil. Christ's route to the cross was marked throughout by a refusal to opt out, and by persevering love. We need this kind of relationship with God and with others – relationships which are more than shallow convenience.

Communion

The compatibility idea begins with the assumption that we are the standard against which others must be assessed, leading to difficulties if others do not fit in with the way we live. Relationships become external, managed, held at a suitable distance. Because the religious focus is inside oneself, there is no hope of deep communion and empathy. Others know they are being held at a distance.

Central biblical truths cut through this individualism. We are not primarily individuals who enter into relationships, but are born and grow in relationships which express who we are. We can be ourselves before God in solitude, but we are to love one another as we love ourselves. And because all of us are problems both to ourselves and to others, the self-satisfaction which comes from a consumer culture is a disastrous illusion. The dethroning of the ego which requires others to be compatible is often painful, but it makes possible relationships where both partners are humble and patient. The partners can be open with each other, accommodate weaknesses and live with irritating habits. The heart of the matter is whether there is an ego-agenda to life, or whether in God's hands we are willing to be shaped to commune with one another.

Chapter 8

OWNING AND BUYING LOVE

Love as possession

One of the great characteristics of love is the giving of oneself to the other. Another person's gift of himself or herself, in whatever way it happens, is the most generous act of all. Paul had this understanding of sexual relationships. Your body is not your own, but you have given it to your spouse, and vice-versa, and so your body's concern is to do what your partner wants. To know that 'my beloved is mine and I am his' is the song of songs. Many, perhaps most, couples experience this process of self-giving as basic to the meaning of love. It is good and right. At weddings, it is symbolized by the transfer of rings which are often seen as tokens of ownership, and it rules out any idea of independence and self-assertion as the relationship develops. Yet this self-giving relationship is, and must be, voluntary; it must be worked out at the time and pace which is acceptable to the one who gives. Because giving, possession and ownership are so important in many areas of life, it is easy to get them wrong in love relationships, and worth spending some time unpacking their meaning.

The question of who owns us highlights the issue. The Christian answer is straightforward: that no person can or should try to own another. God has made us; we are the handiwork of the Creator, but even our relationship with God is not one of ownership and possession. We stand before the Father as children and stewards, but not as slaves. One of Jesus' last messages to the disciples was carefully to convey they were his friends, not his servants. Each of us therefore has our identity and integrity before God as an open relationship. Because God, by creation, owns us, nobody else can. Abraham Kuyper once said, 'When you bow the knee to God, you bow it to nobody else.' Thus slavery is outlawed, parents do not own their children, and marriage relationships are not to be seen in terms of possession and ownership.

Slavery, the business of owning a person, has a long history in the empires of Europe; Greece, Rome, Spain, Portugal, Britain and other countries all fostered slavery. Just as owning slaves has now been recognized as a fundamental denial of personal freedom and dignity, so the idea of owning a wife or husband is basically suspect. It implies that the spouse is treated like a chattel, something at the disposal of the other, to use as the other sees fit. The very idea is repulsive. It is worth nothing that the bride-price, or dowry, which is common in many African countries does not have this character at all. Many studies of the place of dowry in subsistence economies show that this transfer both helps to give resources to older parents and ensures that the husband is capable of providing a livelihood for his wife and children. Its meaning was not usually that of trading goods for a wife. No human being can own another, because only God as our Creator has any such claim on a person; and, as Jesus showed, God's relationship with each of us does not require bondage and servitude, but is intimate and free. The idea of wife as servile possession is still quite strong in some cultures. Women often work far harder than men and are treated as part of the husband's labour force. Much evil is done to women in the name of this view of things.

Another form of the idea is powerful in the West: emotional possession. This is a substitute for faithfulness, the permanent, unconditional giving of one person to another voluntarily from the heart. As couples lose the meaning of faithfulness before God, they try to recreate it through the emotional possession of one partner by the other. Sometimes this is pursued by a process which can be described as buying rather than giving love; behind each act is the agenda which says, '*Now* you will love me, won't you?' At other times it occurs through imposing an emotional leg-iron, creating economic dependence, or other forms of manipulation. Sometimes it is orchestrated through a detailed attempt to control the partner's emotional life; he or she is told all the time what to feel. Viewed subjectively, this is seen as a guarantee of love; it means that this person will never leave me and will remain mine for ever.

Yet it subtly undermines the meaning of faithfulness and troth, because it says to the partner that at the deepest level he or she is not exercising freedom and making a heartfelt commitment. We recognize this in the normal meaning of 'possessiveness'. It implies that the subject does *not* possess the object of his or her affection and desperately seeks to do so, hanging on to the person, whose spirit is elsewhere. The control is external and obsessive and fails to capture the soul of the beloved. In this situation, the partner, feeling smothered and in need of space, might feel the need to withdraw so that he or she can freely give love. Strangely, emotional possession is an admission of the absence of freely given love; it is a substitute which creates further problems.

The solution lies in finding again the basis of freedom, love and trust in relationship with God. The Christian meaning arises from the faithfulness of God to us and the awesome freedom which God gives us to respond in love. Emotional possession is a form of torture to both partners, and it is the birthright of Christians to know steadfast, faithful and freely given love, however inadequate, in their friendships and marriages.

Love as calculation

Another cluster of meanings is linked to the idea of possession in a more twentieth-century sense. While the nineteenth century and earlier saw the idea in terms of the possession of labour, or ownership of the means of production, we in the twentieth see it much more in terms of consumption. Our frame of thinking is not possession as required service but as the satisfaction of wants. Imperceptibly, love has taken on this meaning. We are all used to buying and selling on most days of our lives, and to deciding precisely what our wants and dislikes are. Almost automatically, we can treat love the same way. We trade love for love and each day tot up the accounts. If the account is in debit, we feel peeved and cheated, but when we are in surplus, we feel just fine. Maximizing satisfaction and the calculus of exchange shape the daily intimacies of life. The Beatles were right: 'Money can't buy me love,' but the processes of exchange and the intricacies of cost-benefit analysis have led many people to the opposite conclusion. They believe that the only love they get is the love they will pay for.

Some social and economic theorists have developed this perspective as a general view of human relationships. Exchange theorists in sociology and economics see relationships in terms of transactions through which players seek to maximize their own satisfaction. On this view, our relationships grow out of mean calculations, as we are all very lonely. Some economists even construct complex formulae on the basis of which people are supposed to have another child or an affair.[1] Their mistake is to see this approach as normal rather than as a breakdown of love. When people believe that they must buy love, or will sell it only if they receive a good price, they can no longer give of themselves, or receive from others. Love becomes a process of take and give, a series of transactions in which we calculate what we can get. We have an inner obsession with our rewards, and with what we get out of it. Sometimes, wants develop into needs; the things we need for love become absolute demands which create or can be subject to exploitation.[2] How strongly this contrasts with Jesus' words: 'Give to others, and God will give to you. Indeed, you will receive a full measure, a generous helping, poured into your hands – all that you can hold. The measure you use for others is the one that God will use for you' (Luke 6:38, GNB).

This calculus between couples begins in dating and mating. As the basis for marriage, direct calculations about whether a person is rich or poor are probably quite rare. Yet perhaps there is a range of calculations about whether somebody is a 'good or bad prospect' in terms of earning power. More common is a process of weighing the personal assets of a potential partner against those which can be offered. Sometimes, reflecting this attitude, young men describe a dance as a cattle market or women as 'talent'. Getting the best deal in a relationship, although obviously not love, often shapes relationships strongly. Behind it lurks the implication that when the deal loses its attraction the customer will move on. It is a callous way of approaching a man or woman, which leaves its adherents emotionally dead.

A less direct form of transmuting love into a materialist calculus, however, has influenced many more relationships. Because material well-being has such a high value in contemporary society, the best way of showing love to a spouse seems to be to present them with the material best. Or these things can be seen as a reward for love, just as many shoppers treat themselves and others to rewards.[3] Historically, in an employment market where the career-orientated professional male has dominated, this has been expressed through the man working hard in order, as the saying goes, to provide the wife with all she could possibly want. She has a nice house, and everything within the home is fine, but her husband works long hours and she sees little of him. As he grows more successful, they buy a better house, which normally means that she is stuck further out in the suburbs and away from his place of work. He, because he is successful, experiences even more pressures on his time.

Sooner or later she complains; she resents seeing so little of her husband and decides it is because he does not love and value her. He extends his activity in the area where it is appreciated, namely, at work. When, eventually, the situation becomes impossible, she runs off with a drop-out and he is consoled by his secretary. What is especially sad is that at the deepest level his love was sincere, but, because the materialist culture corrupted it, it was never shared interpersonally, but was always mediated through objects. Many couples who fervently desire a long hug or a romp in bed have to make do with a new kitchen or another holiday in the Bahamas.

117

The calculus view rots many love relationships. When partners begin to ask whether they have got as much from a relationship as they have put into it, acts of ordinary kindness become a focus for bargaining or resentment. 'If you do this for me, I will do that for you' is a disastrous way of proceeding with a relationship. It is also complex. Partners bargain with each other: 'I will probably stop sulking if you stop disagreeing with me. But I am not sulking anyway.' Partners decide what they will trade, and even use what will cause their partner the most pain because it has the highest trading value. The effect of these interactions is to break a relationship down into trading units which can all cause contention. Sooner or later one partner asks, 'Is this relationship worthwhile (for me)?' Because of the terms in which the question is asked, it prompts a negative response.

Lying deep underneath all these attitudes is the ego-satisfaction model which leads to an introverted way of seeing relationships. When people are continually asking what benefits a relationship brings them, it does not leave much room for spontaneous living. When we feel sorry for ourselves, we are apt to remonstrate, 'After all I have done for him . . .!' It is a focus which thinks in terms of commodities and exchange, but which does not recognize the direct interpersonal character of love relationships. In our culture, people who long to give themselves in relationships with one another are being fobbed off with calculations which limit their relationships drastically.

Once upon a time there was a group of workmates who had a glorious Christmas party each year. They gave super presents and had great fun and thanked one another for all they had done for one another through the year. Then a new boss, Clive, arrived. After the first party, when he received a lovely lot of presents, he sent round a memo because he was worried at the expense involved. It said that he had really enjoyed the party, but perhaps next year they should try to cut down on the cost of the presents they exchanged.

Everybody agreed. At the next party, they all brought their

presents. As usual it was a great hoot. When the presents were opened, Peter received a book on *How to Embalm Bodies* and a 1986-vintage bottle of milk. June got a dishcloth with an electric flex attached. Diane was ecstatic with her tin of maggots, running her fingers through them and passing them round surreptitiously. Shirley thanked Dan profusely for turning the tin can inside out and sticking it together again, and Susanna kept 'brushing her hair' with the hairbrush in a bottle. When, finally, Clive was presented with his toilet paper in brine, he was a bit unsure how to respond, but the flushing sound was greeted with fervent cheering. As everybody hugged and parted, they all thanked one another for such a wonderful time and Clive for the great idea, though he wasn't quite sure what was going on.

Love as commodity

Banal though the fact is, love is often seen as a thing which can be bought. Going to the shops and buying the things we want is basic to contemporary experience. We buy an astonishing variety of items because the advertising surrounds them with promises, many of which feed off the importance of love. 'Oh,' we say, 'we're not stupid! We know that!' Yes, but can we escape it? The power of this idiom, driven by the need to sell, lies in its offer of soft toys, cards, cars, kitchens, coffee, holidays, flowers and food as love. Many companies besides Mills and Boon have a vested interest in love.[4] Items may even have a special love mark-up. Who has not bought an extortionately expensive card for a birthday, Christmas or Valentine's Day? And we, poor dudes, pay because it is love. We ask where love is to be found, and, previously, the answer was 'In the eyes of the beloved.' But now love is found in the shopping mall. Young people fall in love and go shopping, unchaperoned as well.

It would be easy to dismiss this as too simple. Yet love is commodity-shaped today. Around the advertising of a fast car, images of love gather. Chocolates, wine, silk clothing and other consumer goods wrap themselves around the meaning of love and tell us that it is here. Women believe they cannot make love without a sun-tan. These consumer idioms entice us with the promise that there love will be found, if we pay. They make love complicated and expensive. It has to be expressed in lavish evenings out and expensive clothes, and misses out on the simple need to talk together. It cannot be love without a bottle of wine and the trappings of affluence. Much of this is described as 'romance' and 'glamour', the process whereby people psych up themselves and their relationships to generate the feeling of love.

But is this really necessary? Perhaps ordinary people are just as interesting and wonderful as 'glamorous' people. Perhaps they are more straightforward, honest and sensitive than those who need to put on an act. Perhaps the sensitive human face is far more beautiful than the over-dramatized, made-up mask. Perhaps the skin, eyelashes and hair of a dear spouse are far more deeply beautiful than the powdered model in a girlie magazine. Thus we face the question whether the ordinary but solemn intimacy of day-to-day, loving relationships is being lost in advertised idioms of love. Somewhere, there must be a man who first beheld his wife in a magazine. 'Hello, she looks nice. Haven't I seen her before somewhere? Just come over here, darling, and let's see what you look like!' Because love is located in things and has been taken over commercially, we no longer believe it can be with us all the time, ordinary, full of fun, and free. But it can.

It was just a look – so easy. Terry had bought Julie fine items of jewellery each Christmas to express his love. They cost a lot and were quality designs. He and she took great care over the clothes which went with them, but the insurance was high and laid down strict conditions. Wearing and looking after them was actually quite difficult.

The look told him what he already knew. Julie needed no jewels. Her beauty was her own, not bestowed by adornment. He did not know how to bring up the subject, but he asked Julie if she liked the necklace. She said she did, very much, and put her hand to her bare throat. When he frowned, she came across and kissed him and said she really *did* like it very much. For once he said what he thought: she was deeply beautiful without jewels. She assessed what he was saying, pointed out that the business of looking after them was quite burdensome, and suggested that they sell them and live a more relaxed life. Terry concurred, happy, as he put it, 'to get rid of the clutter'.

Capitalist love

Within an industrial culture, man–woman relationships often mirrored those which took place within much capitalist industry. The man was in charge and controlled the work of his woman. She was at his disposal to achieve what he wished, and love, to him, meant treating her as a good worker and in a sense paying her her due. The economic dominance of the man in the family, sadly, created the terms of the marital relationship, sometimes even where men were fighting against the evils of capitalism. The power of this model has diminished as work relationships have changed, although it may remain strong among two groups which seem very different – the top business, managerial and professional groups and some old-style manual labouring communities, which still sometimes treat their wives as personal servants. Now, however, the meaning of capitalism has changed; it is more managerial, and ownership is a wider phenomenon. It centres less on ownership of the means of production and more on consumption. The ownership of houses, cars, videos, dishwashers and a new pair of shoes is a major part of life.

Of course, people do not normally treat their partners like dishwashers, although it has been known to happen. Yet love can focus on the idea that 'she is mine'. In some ways this is wonderful. It cuts through all the uncertainties of relationship into the knowledge that this person belongs to me and no-one else, or conversely that I belong to this person and I alone. What a person owns and treasures, he looks after. He lavishes care and attention on it, and frequently takes it out to look again at this beautiful thing that he has bought.

Sometimes women, especially, are treated as such a valuable possession. We scowl at adverts which use women to sell cars, but perhaps ignore the fact that these adverts also define women in terms of cars. Women go well, are fast, make one feel comfortable, are responsive, are turned on, or perform well. Phrases like these reflect the consumption model. The girlfriend is carefully looked after, well dressed and frequently admired. She is seen as valuable, and her value reflects glory on the 'owner'. Behind this lies the assumption that this prestigious possession is simply for his own pleasure. It is uncovered when the woman undertakes independent activities outside the frame of reference which the man has constructed. This threatens him and undermines the terms on which the relationship is conceived. Because people relate to so much around them in terms of ownership and possession, it is easy to transfer these ways of thinking to even the most intimate relationships. Some wives initially enjoy the idea of being 'kept women', not in the sense of being at home and looking after the children, but in the deeper psychological sense of giving themselves over to their husbands to be part of their domain. But sooner or later, as the wife appreciates the implications of what the husband wants as her owner, the fallacy in her loss of integrity becomes evident.

For ten years or so, Barbara had enjoyed marriage, two growing children and a lovely home. She dressed well (colour-co-ordinated) and enjoyed all the goodies which Alistair brought home. But she felt stifled and unfulfilled. Her outside commitment was to Amnesty International. She worked for them three days a week on Far Eastern cases of torture, and developed effective networks to monitor and publicize the cases of injustice. Alistair felt threatened; he was bringing home a very good income and aimed to have everything just so, including his wife. But she was working at, and thinking about, injustices on the other side of the world. He felt he was losing control. He disliked the intensity with which she pursued these cases, contrasted with her relative nonchalance towards the home and their social life.

To bring the issue to a head, Alistair began to discuss the possibility of Barbara getting a paid job. He pushed her quite hard.

'But', she said, 'with your income we can afford me working for Amnesty free; we can contribute to upholding some standards of justice in these areas. If I work for pay, both of us will be saying this justice doesn't matter.'

Alistair agreed, and later realized how close he had come to forcing Barbara to conform to his consumption values. Learning from one's wife was, after all, no great problem.

Consumer culture

The weight of a consumer culture prevents the giving and receiving of love in a yet more immediate way. Earning and buying, calculating and handling goods, leave little room for relationships. Couples spend most of their time together relating through things, and the things themselves even structure the character of the relationship. A dress, a set of golf clubs, a pair of shoes or a carpet becomes an emotionally charged object which generates thunder and lightning. Many of the things we own involve policies which we hold deeply, and, because we are invited to live so fully in a culture of work and the rewards of leisure, differences in our attitudes to things can lead to trauma. Wants and priorities prevent the growth and mutuality of love. They intrude on relationships and claim first place. We spend all the time in the house talking or listening to the inanimate servants and have no time for one another.

Joe found this a problem at meal times. His wife Liz wanted to be thin, but did not want to diet or take exercise. She wanted to buy thinness off the supermarket shelf just like everything else. Or, rather, she wanted Joe to buy it for her because he usually did the shopping. Whenever they sat down to eat, Joe was failing to make her thin. They had fat-free skimmed milk and chocolate digestive biscuits, thin carrot soup and packets of crisps. Joe, who liked to be logical and consistent, could never quite work out what was going on here.

Beyond price

The commercialization of the meaning of love misses the point, and fails to address us as we are. Each person is beyond price, and cannot be owned or treated as a possession. Money never buys real love, and the love of another cannot be possessed. The most we can hope for is the freely given love of another person, and we are all able to give our own love in our own way. But the freedom of love is only part of the situation. Because we are God's, we can belong both to God and to other people. We can give ourselves to them, and they to us, in the exclusive relationship of marriage and in friendships. But it must be on God's terms of non-possessive love and respect. This kind of giving and receiving exposes the possessive person's desire to make the other person 'mine'.

Similarly, the Bible turns upside down the take-and-give calculus of love. That calculus is based upon a fundamental misunderstanding. All of us, even those who suffer deeply, receive more from God and other people than we give. If we operate on a give-take basis, we are always in debt. We face the bankruptcy of our own nature. On an entirely different principle, God asks us to receive unearned life, mercy, grace and love. He also shows us that love confers the greater blessing on the giver. It is more blessed to give than to receive. However ordinary and pedestrian this might seem, because giving truly honours another person, it echoes what we are meant to be. It brings us closer to God and to God's most intoxicating blessings. Christ commanded us to love one another because there is no other way to live abundantly.

We therefore need to be very clear on what money can and cannot buy. 'If one were to give all the wealth of his house for love, it would be utterly scorned' (Song of Songs 8:7) To reinterpret loving relationships in terms of the thought-forms of the market is an insult to God. It is to take our grubby little measures and put them in the scales against the great gifts of God, and in the process demean ourselves. When a woman came and poured expensive perfume over Jesus, the disciples seemed to have a good argument. 'Why this waste of perfume?' they asked. 'It could have been sold for more than a year's wages and the money given to the poor.'

Jesus responded by affirming what she had done. 'She
has done a beautiful thing to me . . . wherever this gospel is
preached throughout the world, what she has done will
also be told, in memory of her' (Mark 14:4–9). And so it is.

Chapter 9

LOVE AS POWER

The problem with romantic love is that we lose control. It takes over and makes us weak and helpless, and then other people take advantage. The powerlessness of love often leads to heartbreak. On the one hand, love reigns powerfully in the lives of some; but, on the other hand, those who do not acknowledge love seem able to ride roughshod over people and come out winners. Millions of men and women have wept uncontrollably because they have been deserted by their partners and feel that the power of their love has been defeated. Things may have gone wrong, but they know that they have given genuine, true love, and it has been thrown away. They have been left unloved, weak, often with dependent children, and teetering on the edge of deep bitterness and hardness. In spite of this, many have continued to love their partners and children, despite the suffering, and have known that whatever the defeat was, it was not the defeat of love.

Yet it is easy, in this situation, for people to harden themselves. Immediately, they are so hurt that they cannot face the grief and inner sense of devaluation and dishonour, but later they address the situation with a new policy. 'I have been caught once, but never again.' They each tell their own psyche that they will never again be open and unconditional in relationships; the base line is mistrust and not love. 'Everybody is out for what they can get, and it is a fool who trusts anybody.' From now on, they will be in control of their relationships, which will be conducted on their terms.

This revolt against love is happening at all kinds of levels in our society. Everywhere there are little notices saying,

'No entry to love; only power relationships allowed here.'
People say it with their offices, wallets and eyes. There are
loveless environments. We all know them and can identify
them. Some architects design buildings without love. When
there are no windows below 10ft, and vents blast stale air at
you as you pass, you know that someone has decided not to
love pedestrians. When occupants of shops and offices are
given no natural light, they know that architects do not like
them. But these 'no-love' decisions and contexts occur at
other levels: in some offices, the men know that if they
'make a pass at' (or, more accurately, sexually harass) a
woman, they will get a stiletto through the shoe. It is open
warfare. Even in very intimate relationships, many people
have decided in their hearts that power is better than love.

Some of those who have suffered find protective havens
of care and love against the hurt they have experienced.
Friendships, refuges, single-parent groups, and women's
and church groups have been built up against the
loneliness of the seeming defeat of love. In these groups,
the recognition of genuine love and its goodness may be
rediscovered, provided there are strong external defences.
But the underlying, nagging question remains: can love be
defeated? In the rest of this chapter, at first indirectly, but
then directly, we shall address the question whether power
is more powerful than love.

The macho male

Machismo is popularly seen as flexing biceps and revving
up motorbikes, but it is part of the great historical identification among men of power as the basis of 'love' relationships. The history is horrific. Men treated women as
conquests, using physical violence and abuse as a way of
bringing them into subjection. They were often territori-
ally confined, subjected to rules and punishment which
would keep them in line, and taught that whatever their
husbands said and ordered was right. Another cultural
form of this idea was that men needed to protect women;
the idea of the knight defending women against external
threats was internalized by both men and women. What

both tended to ignore was the fact that men were protecting women against other men, and often protecting them as their possession. It was in effect a male protection racket. Power was often transmuted into automatic authority, and independent women were regarded as rebellious. Like Katharina in *The Taming of the Shrew*, they had to be brought back into submissiveness. We do not know how widely the threats, abuse, violence and physical domination of women have pervaded our own culture and others. The male conviction that their own power was sacrosanct dominated relationships and ran very deep. Anything which challenged it was threatening.

Yet historically the bases of male power did change. Women moved into the workforce. They became good athletes. Physical violence was publicly outlawed. Possessions are legally shared within marriage. And feminism challenged the idea and practice of male power in institutional terms. Yet still it was difficult to unlearn the idea that love was to be exercised through the use of power. The woman 'needed a boss', and the man who could not dominate was deeply threatened. Many men still cannot see any option other than their own control; their bones tell them this is the way to relate to women.

The pattern runs in families, relationships and the minds of men. The silly sexual myth that women need to be dominated is still producing large-scale physical and sexual abuse. Men control their homes and their wives, becoming petty dictators who cannot let go of their demands and see the bigger picture. At work it surfaces in the idea that the important person is the one who has women at his beck and call; as I was waiting at the airport, there was a loudness and an aura of self-satisfaction around the man who was taking his two secretaries from Michigan to New York for the day to do some Christmas shopping. It is present in the compulsive need of many men to prove themselves as powerful businessmen or sportsmen; their father or someone else had laid down the conditions under which 'You'll be a man, my son', and they have to go and do it. There is also a belief among some men, before and after marriage, that they must prove themselves sexually by what are revealingly described as 'conquests'. Locked up in all these attitudes is the completely inconsistent notion that love has to be strong and powerful, that domination is love. The sheer illogicality of this escapes men who claim to be rational. As a result of the confusion which this view generates, some men actually see abuse and rape as expressions of love.

The egocentric dream which power offers is the idea that if this woman will submit to what the man wants, everything will be all right. When his will reigns, and when she is not being awkward, then peace will prevail. Most potent of all is the emotional closure which says, 'Whatever happens in this relationship, I am going to be in control.' Somewhere, however deeply buried, there is a layer of stainless steel which declares against dependence and openness and for being stronger and impervious to attack. Hence the idiom of the strong, emotionless male. In Hollywood films, macho strength is conveyed through fists, guns, grunts and a firm jaw; and eventually the woman, even if she has a bit of fire, collapses on to him. Sometimes it is seen as sexy. The feminists, more accurately, call it patriarchy.

Many women collude in this view. They duck problems by agreeing that the man is powerful, that he knows best and even that violence is legitimate. They may intend this as love, even though it encourages wrong responses. Other women establish countervailing patterns of power. The public mythology of the sources of women's power is amusing. One source, for example, is said to be the ability to nag, and to produce psychological pressure that will wear down the male in all circumstances. Another is the traditionally female skill of cooking; especially in the era before fast food, men who were hungry would, like Esau, give away anything for a mess of pottage. Then there is the great unwritten history of sexual strikes, where the women withdraw favours to achieve their own ends. Willmott and Young suggest that the wife's relatives and friends can sometimes turn the home into alien territory for the male,

THE MEANINGS OF LOVE

where he is perpetually outnumbered and from which he retreats to the pub.[1] Threats, sulking and many other manoeuvres are used to assert the woman's will. One of the most destructive is the threat to walk out, which leaves the man locked in fear and resentment. Later he comes out with a phrase like 'Anything for a quiet life', and the terms of the power relationship go on. There is often a weary awareness that this situation is not really love, but life is assumed to be like this. There is no real alternative. One learns when to give in and when to assert oneself.

Patrick and Gill fought over it. On the whole, the kitchen and the bedrooms were Gill's domain and she did what she wanted there. Patrick found them too feminine, but put up with them while the main lounge was done to his taste. But the spot over the table was neutral ground. She had dropped his Jackson Pollock, which used to hang there, and had never bothered to repair the glass, explaining that it was out of date anyway. True, the moody poster had seemed all right when he bought it, but it was not the kind of thing he really wanted to live with. Gill frequently covered it with elaborate flower arrangements which, apart from looking good, also said, 'This needs covering up.'

This tapestry was the final battle. Gill showed him into the lounge, and he saw the rich cascade of ochres, browns, greens and reds caught by the sun. It was beautiful; it fitted the spot and had all the marks of Gill's hand. Patrick, trapped by the past, was on the point of saying, 'OK, you win,' when the churlishness of it hit him. He let go, enjoyed her work again and remarked how beautiful it looked. He also knew that this should not be another skermish in a continuing battle, but that his wife's taste deserved his respect.

Those who are subjected to control obviously suffer, often for long periods of time; but the deeper problems reside with those who use power. For they have decided the terms on which they will relate to other people and other people relate to them. Normally, this involves excluding relationships with those who will not relate on the power terms which have been laid down. The rich man will not know, let alone understand, those who do not give a fig for money. The teacher needs to be surrounded by people who will learn. Schoolboys bully those not interested in physical confrontation. But the power-broker is more completely trapped by the terms in which he sees relationships. He has to be lonely, because the control he needs to exercise rules out freely given friendship; and it is not possible to receive help, because help implies weakness. How total is the isolation of the powerful!

This occurs especially when there is physical and sexual abuse. There are several aspects to this problem. One is the well-known phenomenon whereby a person who has been abused in childhood marries someone who is likely to engage in abuse. Although the person who has been abused may collude in the process, the dynamics of the situation may really be driven by the abuser. The person who is addicted to physical abuse seeks out, identifies and pursues someone who has been subjected to abuse and cowed by fear, and remains tied into relating on those terms. Love casts out fear, but those who use fear to construct intimate relationships can know little of love, even if there are those who love them; their thinking travels on the railway lines of control and weakness, and love will be interpreted as weakness.

Behind this lies the poor understanding of those who relate on the basis of domination. They can never know those whom they control. They can never experience freely given love until they untangle it from their power over people. In their desire to fight through life, they cannot even recognize love. Often, too, the love which they especially need is perceived by them as opposition, as when Jesus loved and opposed the Pharisees who were intoxicated with their own power. Thus it is not that power wins, for it loses. Just as the Leninist–Stalinist regimes of Eastern Europe 'won' through the power of tanks, but lost as the empty, brittle shell of lovelessness cracked, so, too, power-based relationships prove bankrupt.

Johnny said that he didn't love Mummy any more. She had smacked him when he had hit Amanda, and he was going to get his own back. At meal time he spat all his food out. Mummy was a bit annoyed when she wiped it all up, and said it was silly. Later, he was hungry, and made noises which Amanda did not like. He was grateful for the milk and biscuits Mummy gave him before bedtime, but he stayed up just to spite her. When she came to kiss him in bed, he pummelled her with his fists and cried, 'I hate you, I hate you.'

He broke as he saw her face, and suddenly admitted, 'I didn't mean to hurt you. I didn't mean to hurt you.' 'No,' she said, 'I know you didn't, but if you try to get your own way, you *will* hurt people. Now will you give me a kiss and a hug?'

Power over love

Rather than replacing love by power, people often try to use love as power. This position is more realistic in recognizing the importance of love in our lives, but, however delicately, it uses love instead of submitting to it. It discovers that the most powerful of all weapons is the withdrawal of love. Old sociology texts used to say that while the working classes punish children with smacks, the middle classes punish them with the withdrawal of love. Perhaps many of us grow up with such experiences. The power of this move is amazing. Suddenly, the one with power no longer has to forgive, be patient and erase the memory of wrongs done. The other person can be repudiated and closed off. Dependence becomes impervious independence. All the weaknesses which are associated with love are removed at a single stroke. Especially if the other person needs that love (and who does not need love?), the position of weakness is replaced by victory.

But, in this game of chess, the final position is now revealed. By using this powerful weapon in a relationship, we actually destroy its power. It is important to see the full implications of this move. God is love and commands us to love; it is the condition of our existence. Those who claim to take control of love, to give or withhold it as they see fit, are playing God and denying the central truth of their existence. If we take the love which the sovereign God shows to us and commands of us, and make it our own petty weapon, we stab ourselves. By asserting power over love, we win, but we lose even that which we would win. Such fools we are!

Like children playing with toy soldiers and guns, we play with this weapon and engage in the temporary withdrawal of love, particularly in order to bring to their senses those who have done wrong, before love is resumed as normal policy. Not only does the weapon become ineffective and destroy itself, however, but also the meaning of love becomes fundamentally misunderstood. Love becomes a namby-pamby phenomenon which comes out only when the sun is shining. It is seen as weak, over against the strength of the hard heart. During bad times it is replaced by scowls, tight lips, withdrawal and coolness, which are deemed to be far more effective. Actually, of course, they are destructive and debilitating, as they are meant to be.

The alternative is love which is critical and committed, which faces what is wrong and sticks with the problem, which sees through the evil and places it in a wider, good context, and which, in Jesus' unforgettable terms, turns the other cheek. Love is capable of lasting through failure. When it is given the controlling role, it has the power to remake situations. It can bring about new understandings. It can persevere through crises to new ways of living and seeing things. Yet we have to be very clear about what this love is. It certainly is not the 'love' which becomes subordinated to, or even dominated by, power relationships which fundamentally assert that one person's will shall be done. Something much more radical is required: love which perseveres and endures, takes no count of wrongs and lives in its God-given power.

Tina felt she had had to fight through much of her life. She had fought at school, with her brothers, and for a decent job. It worried her that she might treat Derek the same way. She knew he was different, and that he was completely on her side; but, whenever she was up against it, she attacked him. It was just words

133

THE MEANINGS OF LOVE

and irritation, but he could always feel it coming and it terrified him. She hated herself for being so aggressive.

One day she was letting fly and felt dominated by the need to fight for everything. But Derek kept on hugging her and asking what he could to to to help. He just ploughed through the verbal arrows, and focused on her and on what she was feeling. She could see his love conquering his fear, and it also defeated her. She couldn't treat Derek as the enemy, because he hung on and was a friend for life, for better and for worse.

After that, she occasionally mounted a few verbal attacks, but there was no heart in them, and they petered out. It interested Tina that she gradually learned to fight *with* people and to establish an underlying commitment to them, which was so different from her upbringing. She discovered that if she fought on the side of the people she met, even if they were antagonistic, relationships were usually for the better.

The use of sex

For those who have abandoned love for sex, there is yet another stage, in which sexual relationships themselves are used in power-directed ways. We have already noted that pornography encourages addictive behaviour, and addiction is linked to weakness and dependence. It is therefore clearly possible for people to use sexual relationships in the same power-based way. There are tales of film stars who have slept their way into top roles, and prostitution has been associated with blackmail down the centuries. But perhaps our concern should be with a more immediate and mundane matter. Many men and women must fear that sex is the only way of keeping their girlfriends or boyfriends, wives or husbands. 'If you won't go to bed with me, how do I know that you love me?' reasons the boy, and she gives way to the blackmail. The wife desperately 'performs', hoping that she can hold on to her man. Or she uses her husband's 'need' for sex to achieve her own ends and purposes.

The competitive use of sex destroys marriages, and what is happening in all these situations is fearful in its destructiveness. For it involves using sex as a weapon to achieve control, exploitation and domination. Sadistic and masochistic practices probably emerge from this view. The Dracula myth represents a horrible version of this attitude. He exercises power over a series of women victims until they are sacrificed to his bloodlust. Before good triumphs at the end, the *Dracula* film invites men who watch it to participate in the idea of total control, and it arouses fear in the women. Many other popular mythical idioms play on and excite the same fears. Underlying all these examples is a meaning of sex which loses its inner connection with love and takes on another agenda. It leaves people hugging to themselves a notion of their own power, and treating their partners in the sexual relationship as enemies to be overcome and dominated. Again the contradiction is frightening. In the act which should signify love and tenderness, patterns of warfare are going on. In these situations, people usually wear underclothes, not armour, and so they are easily hurt.

The big power lie

We now see the fundamental weakness of the view of power which this approach espouses. It is intoxicated by the possibility that control can be established over other people and that they can be defeated when they try to exercise their will independently of the subject. The agenda to which love and sex must bow is 'My will be done', and this distorts relationships and rides over people. It also hardens the hearts of those who choose this master. They have sold their souls to a devil who will destroy them. By contrast, the truth about God's power throughout the whole creation is that it is used for our good, and not against us. This is the astonishing characteristic of Jesus' power. As God, he did not need to be assertive; and, rather than dominate people, he respected the integrity of all he met and worked for their good. Whether by healing, warning or encouraging, Jesus' focus was on what was best for the other person. He showed patience, meekness, long-suffering and steadfastness, and stayed with the people he loved through their problems. This was the gentle power of working for good. This love was not and is not defeated. It can love enemies and persecutors, and can erase the failures of the past with forgiveness. Our guarantee is that even when humankind loved darkness rather than light and killed the embodied goodness of God, God stayed with us. Now many people who have thought themselves defeated in love discover through Christ that God's power of love is far greater than the destructiveness they have experienced. They know that God's love has inestimable power over us and for us.

Chapter 10

LOVE AS ATTAINMENT

Success in love

Those who mix power and love normally have some idea of the contradictions between the principles they have chosen to serve. They do not quite trust love as a sufficiently powerful way to follow, and they therefore opt for an alternative. There is another understanding of love, however, which is seen by its adherents as the only meaning which love can have. It is given by the view which they follow in the rest of their lives, namely a belief in their own achievement and their ability to make their own world. Love here is something one works for and eventually deserves. This is yuppie-culture love. It is for the upwardly mobile. It involves having a successful man at your side, or a glamorous girl on your arm. Love is what human beings create in their own lives, and they do it either well or badly. Just as some people have high salaries and others low, so some people are high achievers in love and others are not. One of the skills of life, therefore, is being successful in love. The process is competitive, like jobs, exams or playing Monopoly. Those who win stand to be congratulated, while the losers have to make do with whatever comes their way. This is both a strong contemporary view and also one with historical roots.

Much of this has to do with the development of the idea of 'career'. A competitive view of work focuses on top jobs which have high rewards. Younger people are encouraged to drive for them through the hope of success and the fear of failure. They are taught to set their sights on what they want to happen, and, when it does, to see it in self-congratulatory terms. Feelings of success, achievement, desert, failure and expectation often become central in the emotional lives of the careerist man and woman. The signs of success are seen to lie in high salaries and affluence. In this context it is quite natural for love to be viewed in the same way. Courtship and marriage are a success story; the signs are, perhaps, having a nice house, an enjoyable time together, children, and a good sex life. Sometimes, of course, it does not actually work out this way. Yet, because it has to be a success story, the cracks are papered over and ignored.

This way of seeing things has a media impetus. The sacred event which typifies the apex of this commitment could be a media award event when the great and the famous arrive in pairs, glowing, fabulously dressed, with their consorts on their arms. The ceremony which follows is an elaborate process of self-congratulation, partly of those who receive the awards, but also of all others who attend the event. The popular media keep up a continual gossip commentary on those who are successful in love, or not. They parasitically feed off great media relationships as if the love of these people were anything other than ordinary.

The converse of this obsession with the success of love is a kind of cruelty towards those who are shown as fallible. A populist reaction has it that those who claim to be successes in love are really just like the rest of us, and mess it up. The media's reports on the latest wedding of Elizabeth Taylor or another star of love are essentially bitchy in conception. Reports on the Prince and Princess of Wales almost seem to suggest that they have let the press down. Thus the media attack that which they create. They frequently print imbecilic horoscopes which include within their platitudes the promise of 'being successful in love'. They continually push the myth and the magic of the love-achievers and play on envy, which is possibly a motive driving this view of the world. As the movie fantasy develops into the Star Wars defence policy, so what is presented on television becomes the model for love.

This perspective also has much to do with class. One of

the problems of the rich and powerful is their continual focus on their own achievements. This has developed in them a need to see love, too, in terms of success. In Britain, debutantes, the daughters of the aristocracy, used to 'come out'. They were thereby entering the marriage market. They would be portrayed in society magazines, and they and their potential mates would attend series of events from Buckingham Palace garden parties to local hunt balls, where the underlying question was who would get whom. The more formal criteria of success involved money, prospects and good looks, but other, less formal, criteria also applied. It used to be common in this culture to refer to women as 'young fillies', employing the language of Newmarket horse sales; or a person was to be congratulated on making a 'good catch'. It was almost a matter of comparing CVs.

Along with this way of seeing things has gone a phenomenon noted by Veblen and others whereby the woman is the man's trophy.[1] Indeed, one theory has it that the elaborate corsetry of the mid-nineteenth century wife was part of a demonstration that she was incapable of work and therefore had many servants – which reflected well on the owner of both wife and servants. This seems a bit extreme, but certainly the women dressed as if they were being displayed on the sideboard. For decades, their long skirts restricted the possibility of any active pursuits. The extent to which this view has constrained the lives of middle-class women and prevented them from being themselves is too well documented to need further comment. Yet it still continues in other forms.

Achievement in mating

In previous eras, choosing a partner was usually defined by where people lived. One married the girl next door, the lass in the church choir, the man in the next office, or the lad from the class above at school. Now the openness of dating is frightening, and those of marriagable age look for categories by which they can order and organize its complexities. One of the most popular is the idea of compatibility, which we have already examined; but another, perhaps even more influential, is the idea of success in dating.

Its first expression is sometimes referred to as 'scoring' with the opposite sex. It is often meant sexually, and, as we saw in the previous chapter, there is a well-established but very destructive sub-culture within which young men (especially) believe that their prowess and popularity are established through sexual 'conquests'. Love has little or nothing to do with this; it is more akin to taking scalps, and is characterized by a shallow or non-existent appreciation of relationships. A similar idea is that of flirting. Sometimes this is simply attention-seeking, but often it means a competitive use of sexual chemistry to achieve the end the person has in mind. It involves the use of seductive techniques, dress, attention-drawing motifs, cosmetics and images which project the individual. Magazines are full of them, and so is our culture. Take for instance an article which claims that bald men are sexy. On what grounds? It might be based on the idea that sexual activity makes one's hair drop out. Clearly, this is an area where fantasy, whether by bald men or by women, leads the mind. It is part of the mythology of sexual achievement. Yet those whose identity rests in their sexual attractiveness often set out on quests which are disastrous for both themselves and others. They suffer because their identity is so narrowly based and so dependent on unstable relationships. Others suffer because they are used and exploited in relationships which are fundamentally unconcerned with them. They are merely a foil for the seductress or the woman-slayer.

A more ordinary form of this view sees mating in terms of making the best possible match. Relationships are conceived in terms of the qualities of various potential partners and what each can offer the subject as a reward. In our culture, achievement is measured in terms of education, status, money, strength, appearance, popularity, and many other, less tangible characteristics such as a sense of humour, good manners, a sense of fun, and personality. The understanding is that love is achieved by getting the best possible mix of these criteria. Potential mates are therefore assessed very carefully to see what they offer and how this compares with the assets which the subject has to offer. Dating is a bit like the Stock Exchange, with bids and counter-bids, offers and trading, until a merger is finally negotiated. The mode of attraction remains external. It is represented by a thousand corny images in which the guy plays a great game of football and the girl falls wide-eyed on his neck. During this period both partners are under pressure to advertise all their best features and to hide their worst. Then, when the deal is clinched, the appearances can be discarded. If the problems of this presentation stage are overcome, a deeper scenario is revealed as each partner faces what the other is really like.

There is an interesting convention of dating which seeks to avoid this competitive attitude in which one person is compared with others. People are not comparable, and marriage is not a matter of shopping for the best bargain. In courtship, the norm is to pursue one relationship through to marriage or to friendship rather than to engage in a comparison of potential partners. It is a wise practice which many people follow automatically. Those who do not might ask themselves whether they are enslaved by the idea of successful dating.

What happens when people present themselves as a good catch? Some sincerely believe that they *are* a good catch and are therefore likely to make judgments about other people who are not up the mark. Others are not quite so sure, and become concerned with creating a good impression. They might feel that being liked and loved is something they have to work at. The internal cost is a fear that they will not be loved unless they are attractive. This is especially a problem if pretence and self-presentation have played a part in the formation of a relationship. They fear that they must be fun, dynamic, successful or seductive if love is not to die. Sometimes the fear is entirely subjective; it occurs despite the unconditional love of the partner. The woman wonders whether he will still love her with these wrinkles. He fears the loss of his job, his aura of success and his ability to make money, because he is not sure whether she will love him any more if they disappear. Tragically, on becoming unemployed, more than one man has left wife and family because he feels he has let them down. The scenario invites love to remain focused on externals, on performance and on whether each partner has a good deal.

Failure

Another aspect of this attitude is the way in which it leads people to look at themselves. There are areas in the lives of all of us where we fail. If we are driven by the compulsive desire to succeed, however, these areas must be sublimated and buried, for they cannot be loved. But it is precisely this move which makes simple problems intractable. For example, our culture leads us to believe that men must be successful with money. They must flaunt a roll of bank-notes, a fat wallet or many credit cards. Achievement is often linked to high spending, and some men bluff. The failure to handle money well is then covered up by pre-tence until the man and his partner suffer deeply for the self-deception. The idiom requires us to ride on success. Underneath, all the time, is the fear which leads failure to be buried, making it inaccessible to love. This weakness has trapped many couples and left them unable to address their problems.

Anita was worried more than she had ever been before. The courtship had been exciting. She was vivacious, and enjoyed the evenings out and planning the marriage. It was a continuation of college and her time at the Inns of Court when she had continually enjoyed the *frisson* of life and the fountains of success. She had no doubt of Ben's love, but marriage had meant moving into another world – home, housework, ordinariness and defeat. She remembered her mother and the impression she gave of not really being anything. Anita had wanted to escape from this for years, and now it was going to trap her. She wanted to share this fear with Ben, but couldn't, because he had not married a frightened housewife. The fear was related not just to her mother, but also to housework; you could pass exams, but untidiness always attacked

142

you again. So she bluffed, but with moods of depression which frightened Ben because they were so inexplicable to him.

Curiously, the first pointer out of the depression came after a visit home. She suddenly saw Mum in a different light. She wasn't anything, but she didn't need to be. There was a lack of hype, which Anita found she had come to need. She hugged her Mum, thanked her for all she had done at the wedding, and felt a bit more in touch with herself. Later, when she and Ben cooked the evening meal together, he burned the saucepan. It seemed a crisis, but it was soon cleaned up, and the rest of the evening was very pleasant.

Another related attitude is the decision that some men and women make to withdraw respect from their partners when they fail. Sometimes there seem to be grounds for doing this – drunkenness, unfaithfulness, weakness, aggression, or serious criminal behaviour. Yet these actions may represent only a small part of a person's life, and the judgment is harsh because it fails to honour fully who the person is. Most withdrawals of respect are based on criteria which are limited by the viewpoint of the judging partner. She decides that his manners are not good enough for polite company, and disowns him. He decides that she talks a lot of nonsense and should not be with him in public. She decides that he lacks taste; he that she looks dowdy. Such withdrawals of love do, however, point to the kind of love that must have been there originally. At first it involved a set of judgments which concluded, 'You are worthy of me,' and this conclusion was later changed into the statement, 'You are not really worthy of me.' Thus we can see the destructive effects of the underlying attitudes of self-glorification and self-assumed status. The self-congratulation of many relationships produces its own mouldy fruit, and real love remains the experience of the humble.

When Alex and Belinda met, she was rather taken with his friends. They were fast-talking, high earners, and full of fun, and had an incredible social life.

143

After they became engaged, she realized that she and Alex were seeing far less of them. One of the very things she had liked him for was no longer there. One evening they discussed it. Alex told her that the whole group had exploded. Recently, quite a few of them had lost their jobs in the recession and didn't want to be around any more. But he suspected that many of the others were like him; he was fed up with the artifice, sexual envy and posturing of the group. The need to be successful wasn't leading anywhere and just made relationships tiresome. He was glad when he met Belinda and they had been able to develop a good, honest relationship, free of all that stuff. When she next met members of the group, she received a couple of catty remarks which conveyed how accurate Alex was.

The rewarding relationship

Along with the focus on the high-achieving individual goes an emphasis on a rewarding relationship. Some people are popular because they are pleasant and good people. But sometimes the idea of popularity contains another idea. The rich, the famous and the powerful offer rewards which are sought by others. Webs of achievement are woven around sets of people, many of which are at least tinctured by self-congratulation. What these groups have to offer may seem alluring from the outside. Some relationships follow a similar pattern. Especially if we have a sense of void, what another person has to offer can seem so great. Yet because the internal structure of this relationship is built on what we lack, and on hopes and aspirations for ourselves which we have not fully faced, it is not likely to work well. Such responses need to be opened up and shared, particularly in courtship and marriage. 'You always seem so at ease with everybody.' 'I'm not really much fun.' 'You are so much more intelligent that I am.' This way of thinking is misplaced, and over-values these characteristics. Intelligence, for example, involves different kinds of thinking, some of which most people have, or can develop. What is experienced as inadequacy is often just a different balance of talents and qualities. Each of us can give a great deal, and we always give more than mere intelligence or a sense of humour.

How then can we decide whether we are having a rewarding relationship? There is a perverseness in the process, for those who set out to grab the rewards seem to find that either they do not come or they are empty when they do. The career achievement of a partner, which seems so important at one stage of life, is merely something that makes him late home at another. The glamorous woman eventually becomes a slave to her need for beauty. Events planned as part of a rewarding relationship often turn out to have a hidden flaw. Specific occasions may have their glow, but 'reward' is too instant and superficial an idea to convey what is really involved in relationships. If the rewards come only from the things we achieve in a relationship, then they do not touch who each person really is.

A similar question is whether one person can be more rewarding than another. The very concept is so wooden. When two people live and grow together for forty or fifty years, they are forming one another anew each day, week and month. The richness lies in the growth of each person in love, beauty, wisdom and purity. Any achievement which is worthwhile will come from these deeper qualities anyway, and will be based on cooperation and mutuality. To fix the vision of love on some supposed reward offered by various characteristics sticks in the shallows.

Rewards or blessing, but not both

'Blessing' is a far better word than 'reward'. It identifies the fact that deep, strong relationships arise not from pursuing rewards, but from giving oneself in a way which is pure and depends on God's unpredictable response. Many good relationships rely on, and can only happen through, suffering. 'Blessing' also underlines the sense that relationships should be good and wholesome. They should produce fruit. This can happen only if the real focus for each person is love and care for the other. The underlying fallacy of the 'achieving' focus is in the reference-point – itself. It clings to the idea that individuals are capable of engineering their own rewards. This involves ignoring how heavily everyone depends on what they are given by others

– by their parents, teachers, friends, nation, church and forebears. In particular it fails to recognize how insubstantial are the achievements of any of us, and how they turn to chaff when we believe only in ourselves. Finally, it fails to recognize its total dependence on God's grace, which goes on when the performance stops, and does not merely count achievement and success, but is given to all of us when we cannot offer anything of worth.

Joan was always slightly angry with Arthur, although she loved him. She was quite clear about the reason. She felt she should have married somebody better. Just before they had met, he had decided to be an ordinary family doctor and not to go into surgery or hospital work. She expressed her irritation occasionally but regularly, through odd comments, although it did not really matter any more.

She went to the health centre to give him a lift home, and as he came out of his surgery door he spoke to a young mother who was next in the queue. She leapt up, hugged Arthur and told him that the baby was fine. Joan froze. It was not that there was anything improper in the act; it was just that her love and gratitude to Arthur were unconditional, while she, Joan, always lived with a reservation, even in far more intimate situations. She realized that things must change. She arranged with Arthur that she would come back in twenty minutes when he had seen the remaining patients.

Chapter 11

THE ROOT PROBLEM

The story so far

These chapters were written by a sociologist keen to understand what is going on in man–woman relationships today. As such, the book is an exploration, because this is one of the most difficult areas to study. Although some research is relevant, few family studies and social surveys which examine sexual attitudes engage fully with the questions of love which are considered here. People may make statements about love, but these often depend on the views of others, and it is not easy to see how much they are their own. Magazines, novels, television and films continually represent love, often without words. The domain of study is vast. A bigger problem occurs because it is quite difficult to know what even our friends think about love. It is too vast and personal a subject. It involves all of us closely, and many of us cannot even articulate what is happening at certain stages of our own lives. In this area it is easy to destroy what is touched. This study therefore relies on exploring a set of meanings of love. It uses sources, cultural and personal, which present meanings current in our daily lives. It is allusive, in suggesting to readers areas in which they might have had experience of these meanings, and invites readers to discern whether and how any of the analysis might be relevant to their own relationships. In this sense it aims to be directly personal, and remains suggestive.

But this question is not only personal, but also cultural. Although many people might feel that their own experience of love is unique, they take part in broader social movements which are deeply formative. One question raised by the various meanings of love presented here is whether they dwell in people's minds and hearts. It is possible to analyse them further, but broadly they seem to be empires which can claim a lot of loyal subjects. Happiness, feeling and duty are conurbations in which the traffic of love gathers. Each of them has its own logic and language, and expects people to pay taxes in its own currency. Mapping this wider cultural territory has therefore been the main task of the preceding chapters. They suggest the overall geography of love in the last few centuries, with, one hopes, some accuracy. Yet this analysis was undertaken to answer a question: *why has love so often failed?*

This, too, is a deeply personal question for many of us. Why does love fail in our relationships? As mentioned at the beginning of the book, the personal question is too extensive to address fully here. Other family, personal and faith issues are likely to be significant. Yet the subject-matter of this book does allow one kind of answer which may be important to a lot of people. *Our love fails because it is the wrong kind of love*. The kinds of love we have examined have faults written into their design. Many people enter relationships with genuine commitment and a full-blooded determination to love, but things seem not to work out. This may be because we are wedded to views which thwart these hopes. Part of the analysis in earlier chapters was concerned with opening up these problems so that they can be seen more clearly. If this is indeed a substantial part of the answer to the question, it should help us in our relationships to love more truly.

We should note that it is no purpose of this exploratory analysis to undermine all the genuine love which is expressed in people's daily lives. Real love is straightforward, and is marked by patience, kindness, a lack of envy and a desire for the other's good. It does not depend on reading books; it makes the world go round, and brings people into contact with God. Young and old, those with abilities and disabilities – everyone can love at any time. Even when love is intended, but does not work out as it should, it remains real, and it was continually honoured by

Jesus. Thus, although this book makes cultural judgments about certain models of love, it should not be used as a source for judgmental attitudes in particular relationships. The models will only partially fit, and they could obscure love which needs nourishing.

Perhaps many of us are too close to the problems of our own love, and could profitably reflect more on our cultural location. Never before in the history of the world has the culture of a generation been so shaped by the media and education. Previous generations learned about love in the context of a few key relationships which they experienced as they grew. The people they lived with had views on how to live and love which largely framed their own responses. Now, for twenty, thirty, forty or more hours a week, children and adults receive teaching from the media, which convey among other things how they should view love. But it is transmitted as dogma; through images, drama and incidental messages the media say, 'This is what life is like.' There is no other way of seeing things. The meanings presented in earlier chapters are widespread media idioms which are not held up to question. We are a generation which has been taught to love as no other, and often by those who have no real interest in the subject, but wish to use it for commercial ends. If we have been falsely taught, there is a need for some fundamental relearning. A mass culture can be comprehensively wrong. It may claim to be harmless, but if it has given false answers, we are dupes if we follow them.

Shoots from the same root

Our culture has first offered models of love and then recorded their failure. The earlier chapters of this book looked at older models such as ideal love, romantic love and love as happiness. Those models involved and contained within them an optimism about the fruits of love. They rang with the hope of a forward-looking culture. If our analysis is approximately correct, this optimism foundered on the weaknesses which these views contained. As each generation pushed further the implications of viewing love this way, they produced more bitter fruit. Later views of love, focusing on attainment, power, consumption and compatibility, had fewer pretensions. Some of their adherents would not even talk about love. They were part of a post-romantic culture. They were worldly-wise and even cynical. This post-romantic culture has come to the conclusion that love is a failure. It does not work. It lets people down.

Yet the glaringly faulty logic of this conclusion has been exposed. What we have been examining in the past chapters has been the failure of certain kinds of love. But if, as we suggested, they are flawed views, it was inevitable that they should fail and let down the people who were influenced by them. This is only the failure of these kinds of love, not the failure of love itself, and especially not of Christian love. Yet we are now in a position to ask why these failures have taken place and whether they have something in common.

There is an answer which lies under the ground which we have already raked over. All these meanings which we have examined have grown out of post-Enlightenment humanism. This term needs explaining. It means not a narrow ideology or set of ideas, but an underlying religious conviction that humankind is the source of its own meaning and can discover its own truth. Since the eighteenth-century Enlightenment, western culture has in part pursued the idea that the worship of humankind is the best contemporary faith; each of the views we have examined puts something human at the centre of the universe and of the meaning of love. All the views have turned away from finding the truth about love in God, and have sought it in various human ideals and hopes. Human feelings, happiness, duty, achievement, satisfaction and compatibility dictate the outworkings of love. If there is something wrong with these perspectives on love, it suggests that the root faith in humanity as the source of love is suspect.

Is this the case? Can we trust this humanity? Or, more personally, can we trust ourselves? This is not just trust in a day-to-day sense, but in the deeper sense of allowing a faith in humankind to define the meaning of love. The answer has to be 'No' – not just because we recall the millions of deaths which occur each year because of human evil, or because we recognize the scale of the failure of love in which we have all participated, but because none of us can put our trust in what comes out of our own hearts. Our love is a failure; it is compromised both in conception and by the way we live. Even our ideals are corrupted. This faith has fed on the optimistic hope that the next definition of love, the next trial of romantic love, will work. But it does not. The flaw is that it trusts the creature rather than the Creator. Now the basic falsehood of this faith becomes evident: our own faith in ourselves and in our ability to construct the meaning of love cuts us off from any possibility of rooting out the problem. *We* are the problem. That in which we have faith is the problem. The policeman we have brought along to solve the mystery of the murder of love is himself the murderer.

In order to reflect on this central question, let us look at six different ways in which the meanings of love generated in our post-Enlightenment culture have damaged and hurt relationships, moving from the least to the most serious.

First, we have scarcely noticed the changes which have happened to love. It would take a lifetime of quiet watching to begin to see the pattern clearly. The way in which people now talk about love is confused. There is a disintegration in words such as 'faithfulness' and 'lust', which previously did good service, and couples have to put together their own meanings of love as they select from the smorgasbord we have previously set out. This faith has fragmented language and meaning into a post-modern world of relativized values. The seeming impossibility of trust is postponing many marriages, and couples who try to live with several different versions of the meaning of love are often at sea without a compass. In this book we have separated out the various meanings of love in order to examine their direction, but this ploy creates a false sense of order, because they are all experienced as a daily babble, claiming allegiance and spreading confusion.

Secondly, each of the models of love presented is internally defective; it fails. It takes some focus of faith in humankind and makes it the core meaning of love. Yet what it puts its trust in is either mistaken or partial. The 'ideal' is a self-generated creation which is imposed on the other person; it feeds our weaknesses into the relationship. The conception of love as power reflects our misunderstood need for control, and the breakdown of trust. And the idea of sex as pleasure, seen as so good and creative by its adherents, harms and dehumanizes many of those used by it. It is not just that the concepts are defective, but that their falsehood leads to evil. The untruth is lived out by young men and women who suffer and are hurt, albeit often willingly. The tender relationship of sex becomes rape. A love relationship becomes a fight. Or a romantic attachment demeans a wife and children. These defective meanings also distort people's inner lives. They are torn by conflicting feelings, duties, ideals and ambitions. There is no peace in the routes they offer, because the meanings address only a bit of life. To respond to feelings, attainments, bodies, duties or wants is only part of being human and of loving. These meanings let their adherents down, both as individuals and in relationships.

Thirdly, each of the models locates its faith either in the subject or in the other person. It introduces a polarity into the meaning of relationship. We can put faith in our own ego and believe that we find there the meaning of life, but this reduces our partner to the level of an instrument. Or faith can be founded in the beloved, who is idolized and becomes the source of the lover's identity. This is a choice common to many of the models we have outlined. Either people's egocentric ideals imprison their partners, or their romantic ideals enslave them. Either her feelings dominate him, or his define the moods of her life. In each case the fundamental conditions for relationship are undermined. If the meaning of life lies with the subject, then the other person is external and instrumental to that meaning. If the other person is the meaning of love, however, then the subject's identity has meaning only in relation to the partner. The inner ground for a mutual relationship of equal respect and integrity is broken. Either (in Sartre's words) 'Hell is other people', or we have a dependent identity. Millions of us have learnt to think egoistically in dozens of daily thought-patterns which ensnare us in false meanings of love. Or we are trapped in a faith in the partner which will let us down. In both cases our love is doomed by its failure to recognize how central is the biblical command to love the other as we love ourselves. Neither person is to be idolized, and both are to be respected. We are persons in relationship; not individuals first, or worshippers of others, but children of the living God.

Fourthly, and more seriously, this trust in humankind, however it is expressed, cuts us off from what is good. Part of our culture is the idea that we are all good guys really, and most of us find it hard to believe that we actually create evil. Yet, individually and in relationship, we do produce evil; the evidence is around each one of us. Most of us daily add to the sum of evil in the world; we are mixtures of indifference, love, faithfulness, hatred, selfishness, deception and weakness. But the mixture cannot be separated like oil and water; it is more like the mixture created by sugar, salt, pepper and soot. Even our good commitments are partially corrupted by our bad, and, if we trust in them, then we are trusting what is defective. We have seen this in model after model which has turned out to be defective: duty which blames, happiness which ignores, achievement which is proud and feelings which attack. We have set out with hearts bursting with love and good intentions, and have produced something that is bad all through.

Maybe we need to take the problem of our evil more slowly. Most of us think of quick patch-up jobs, a rapid change of policy or an explanation which firmly locates the problem somewhere else. But this problem is pervasive, intestinal. It is not easily externalized. Unless the analysis in these chapters misses the point, we are most seriously mixed up. Nor is it easy to find a good bit of us which we can trust, an island we can climb on to while we drag our other failings out of the water. We are swimming in the problem all the time. In fact the only way out seems to be to stay in the water. The apostle John stated it more authoritatively: 'If we claim to be without sin, we deceive ourselves and the truth is not in us. If we confess our sins, [God] is faithful and just and will forgive us our sins and purify us from all unrighteousness' (1 John 1:8–9). In this sense, there is no good in us. We need some way of developing an awareness which can address our failings and allow us to separate salt and soot before they become so fully mixed. Only when we have a sure place to stand outside our self-deception and failings can we see ourselves with discernment.

Fifthly, these models of love narrow its meaning. Jesus addressed this problem. The Pharisees and others around him focused on limited understandings of love. Those who believed in attainment saw a poor widow putting two small coins in the temple treasury, and thought, 'That's not much.' Jesus saw it and perceived the richness of her heart, the openness of her giving and the real value of what had been put in. He saw how people ignored the love built into the creation and clouded it with meanness. He showed how love could forgive and free people, heal them and make them friends. He demonstrated that love was far wider than having sex or liking people, and that it could define every relationship. In our era, love has increasingly been seen as involving sexual transactions, feelings or material benefits such as having a good holiday. It is being closed down and made redundant because our own conceptions are so narrow. We no longer see that it is possible for love to characterize most of our significant relationships. Jesus brings these attitudes under judgment as fundamental mistakes in human understanding, and opens the boundaries of love. We can love anybody anywhere – we can blow kisses at traffic lights or say 'After you!' in the rush hour.

Finally, the overwhelming mistake in all these views is that they have persuaded people to turn their backs on God and seek their own ways and meanings. We have seen enough to suggest that these meanings are counterfeit. But we grab hold of error only when we have lost our hold of truth. If the truth of love exists not in opinions or human constructions, but in God's relationship with us, then our culture has started in the wrong place. How could this have come about? Perhaps the most astonishing event of all history is the reaction of the cultural leaders of the day to Jesus. No reader of the gospels can easily avoid the conclusion that this man – healer, teacher and friend of the weak – was overwhelmingly good. Yet the leaders hounded him to death. The light shone in the darkness but the darkness did not understand it. The human ability to miss the point is way beyond what most of us believe. We tend to assume that people occasionally get a few ideas wrong; we do not believe that we and others are deeply perverse. Yet these constructions about love are, many of them, perverse; they succeed brilliantly in coming to the wrong conclusion. Of course, the reader may be free from this perversity. Or it may be present, at base in a determination not to recognize God as the source of love and its meaning.

We can see love in the way God has created each of us, the care which was lavished on the design of our eyelashes, tastebuds and immunity systems, the fact that we are provided with parents, and in the sky which greets us each morning. We can see it in the precepts given for our daily life, showing how we are meant to live and love. We can see it tested in the life and teaching of Jesus. Then we learn that love is given by God, rather than being self-inspired. The strength of our love therefore needs to lie with the gentle power of God. Self-generated love and its own meanings get no further than its own weak terms of reference; by contrast, living in response to God is the way to live in love.

These six weaknesses of human models of love are played out daily in our culture, and we all suffer the consequences. The scale of this failure is frightening, but it can be recognized only if we are prepared to examine ourselves critically in relationship to God. The humanism in our culture will continue to say that there is no problem. So, when we ask, 'What is the way to love?' we listen to the man who answered, 'I wouldn't start from here.' There is a better place to start.

My failed love

This is not just a great cultural failure, but also an individual one. It often feels very complicated. As Tolstoy said in the first sentence of *Anna Karenina*, 'All happy families resemble one another, but each unhappy family is unhappy in its own way.' Sin is complicated; no less so when it occurs within love. Basic problems hang around and generate subsidiary ones such as sleeplessness, depression and fatigue. Nor is it easy to unravel the knot of a relationship's history. Going back to the place where something went wrong is only part of the task, for all kinds of things may have followed from the initial problem. Yet there are a number of moves which are central to constructing a relationship of love.

One is an awareness of the failure of our love. Each of us, in declaring our love, often also trusts in it. Yet it is often a weak plant living in poor soil. To recognize these weaknesses is to deepen our commitment. The trust belongs with God, and from the soil of God's good Word we grow out of failure.

Another move is to rediscover our integrity before God. We are often strung out on feelings, sexual urges, our own elation or depression, and what we want from life. These pull us in different directions and there is no centre to our lives. We need to allow all these dimensions of our life to come back into relationship with God, to dwell in our personhood before God.

> But I have stilled and quietened my soul;
>   like a weaned child with its mother,
>   like a weaned child is my soul within me.
> *(Psalm 131:2)*

We have also to throw away many levels of self-obsession. We are concerned with our love, success and feelings. Minute by minute our thought processes focus on ourselves and fabricate visions in which we are god or goddess. In

Christ's unforgettable words, 'Whoever wants to save his life will lose it, but whoever loses his life for me . . . will save it' (Mark 8:35). This process of losing our life and 'our' love is the only escape from our egocentricity.

Another task we must undertake is to learn the language of genuine, heartfelt love. This involves starting with the simple things. Our great gestures of making love had best begin with praying, cooking, listening, and waiting for the one we love. Big gestures are no good when they do not fit with daily care and concern. The truth (or otherwise) of our love cannot be hidden from God, or really from one another. Like Peter after he had denied Jesus, we are given the opportunity to say, 'Lord, you know all things; you know that I love you' (John 21:17). As we move from mixed motives to the simplicity and openness of heartfelt love, the transparency of love will emerge in our relationships with one another.

Above all, we learn of Christ and open our lives to God so that the central highway of love in our lives is open to traffic. We shall spend more time investigating this in the final chapter.

Chapter 12

ANOTHER WAY

Much of our love is reactive; we give love because others give it to us. Or the relationships we have around us demand love; they expose our previous failures and demand something better, something more obviously true. And yet the truth of love does not dwell in our hearts. Our love is compromised and often quite pathetic. This is not because we do not want or intend to love, but because it does not work out in the context of all the pressures and attitudes which clog our arteries. And, more than that, it is so complicated. Handling and responding to these meanings leads to convolutions which cannot be understood. We think about love in bed, on the train, in the car, and as we watch television, and it does not seem to work out. We are flippant, cynical or emotionally cool; we suppress the questions, live with compromise and failure, or just suffer privately. The way out is not straightforward either. These patterns are rooted deep in our lives, and they need to be converted into something different, which will make love normal and strong rather than an aberration.

Christian love

The transition is a massive one. It means moving away from egocentric visions of love to one which lays hold on the love of God and recognizes it as the core truth of life. Here is the central truth to which our failings can be tied and which enables us to assess all the twists and turns of this book's earlier chapters. God's love is not an idea or a feeling, but the very ground of our existence which is manifested in what we daily experience. This truth reinterprets us, so that we see ourselves and our relationships with hair-splitting clarity.

The first thing that strikes us is the sheer scope of God's love in our lives. There is the care invested in the creation – in the cellular structure of a blade of grass, the oxidization of minerals, or the construction of our digestive systems. There is the glory of each morning, and of the exquisite variations of a bird's song; its feathers also lavishly display a creative brilliance. The creation delivers food, and more exotically than as a packet of knitted protein. It comes as mangoes, celery, beef and wholemeal bread. The rain falls on the just and the unjust. The so-called problem of evil has a very simple answer. God continues to love those who are evil, despite the wrongness of their actions. That love is direct, personal, open and non-manipulative, and can be seen by the straightforward way Jesus treated those around him.

The sheer transforming vitality and variety of Jesus' love is amazing. It led a woman to throw herself at his feet in public, and to kiss and cry over them and wipe them with her hair. And he, although 'defiled' in the eyes of the onlookers by allowing a prostitute to touch him, honoured her above those onlookers (Luke 7:36–50). He loved a rich but despised little man who was trapped by his wealth; he received his hospitality and transformed his outlook. Zacchaeus then breathed a generosity which had shrivelled in his lungs before (Luke 19:1–9). Jesus healed a man who was deaf and dumb, so that the man's friends were overwhelmed with amazement. Their testimony was: 'He has done everything well' (Mark 7:31–37). Twenty centuries before feminism he saw two women in their preoccupation with housework, and freed them to recognize the importance of their full relationship with God and what they could learn about living in it (Luke 10:38–41). He was known and criticized as the one who was a friend of prostitutes, drop-outs and those who collected taxes for the hated Romans, but he never exploited them or showed them disrespect. They enjoyed his company and returned his love. He travelled a long way to meet the insane and cure them of their affliction, and worked to the point of exhaustion to heal young and old. He did not select his students on the basis of intellectual qualities or wealth, but taught each of them personally that they were God's children (John 1:12–13). And the children loved him. The adults told them off for praising God in the temple (as Jesus had told them they could), but Jesus honoured and welcomed the children and made them well (Matthew 21:14–16). This man gave blessing, told the truth, and never sought his own advantage; yet he was hounded to death.

Jesus, in his love, understood people, and especially their distorted motives and weak attitudes. He recognized that many of those following him were after bread or a new miracle and were not really engaging with him, and yet he did not respond with bitterness or cynicism (John 6:26–35). He encouraged every sign of love, however weak. He never laid burdens on people that were not light and easy (Matthew 11:29–30). He took people through failure. And his love was tested to suffering – travelling to see people, being hated by the powerful, and eventually being crucified through totally unjust procedures. This situation he met with the words: 'Father, forgive them, for they do not know what they are doing' (Luke 23:34).

His reaction to Pilate was even more acute. Pilate had Jesus beaten and attacked with thorns to show who was boss. In the subsequent interview Jesus made allowances for Pilate, recognizing the pressures on him which came from Rome and the Jews. It is the little things which demonstrate Jesus' love. When Judas was setting out to betray him, Jesus knew what was going on, and could easily have made a fuss, manipulated Judas' feelings, or used his position of power to stop him. What he actually did was to warn in general terms about how terrible it would be for the person who did such a thing, giving Judas the opportunity to change (Matthew 26:20–25). Then Jesus explicitly gave Judas permission to go and do what he intended to do, but without conveying to the other disciples what was involved, so that Judas would not be subject to retaliatory behaviour. The disciples thought he was going to do some shopping (John 13:21–29).

Central is Jesus' commitment to love through sin and failure, and to establish the triumph of love over them through atonement and forgiveness. So God's love to us is steady – not hitting back, not vindictive, not returning evil for evil, but making the sun shine on bad and good alike, loving enemies and turning the other cheek (Matthew 5:38–48). As Christ showed us, God's love is uncompromisingly *for* us all the way.

It also addresses us as a command. This is because we were created to love. The central truth about ourselves and our relationships is discovered as we love our neighbours, and especially our partners, as we love ourselves. This is no external command, but expresses what we are truly meant to be. This central respect for ourselves and others in full personhood is the place where our true meaning is revealed. This love banishes fear and hatred and opens up the longings and questions of the heart. Even when we fail, it comes back with a gentle insistence that we obey the command to love. When we feel wronged 'seventy times seven' times, we are still commanded to love. This is, as Christ has demonstrated, the ground of our being.

It is also fully personal, involving every aspect of our lives. We are to love the Lord our God with all our heart, soul, mind and strength, and so we are to love our neighbour, husband or wife (Matthew 22:37–40). Love incorporates body, hunger, health, emotions, relationships, rest, truth, peace, faithfulness and hope. This is evident in all kinds of incidents in Jesus' life, which showed that he loved people where they were at. If they needed food, healing, forgiveness, respect, comfort or criticism, that was what they received. The disciples learned the pattern from Jesus. When a crippled beggar asked Peter and John for money, Peter answered, 'Silver and gold I do not have, but what I have I give you. In the name of Jesus Christ of Nazareth, walk' (Acts 3:6). This is love with awareness. It listens to what the other person is saying. It discerns the need. It prays for understanding and wisdom, and it puts others in the full light of God's purposes for their lives. It takes pleasure in what is good for the other person.

The focus is the other person and his or her good. Many of our perceptions of what is good for others are tainted with our pride and sin. We think we are good for someone when we are not, and our love becomes mythical and ineffective. Jesus penetrated through layers of immediate needs, such as food and healing, to the central needs of those he met. The thief dying alongside him on the cross was able to face up to his wrongdoing, address his own death, trust Jesus and know with certainty the promise of eternal life (Luke 23:39–43). While on the cross Jesus gave John to his mother as an adopted son who would provide a home for her in Jerusalem and share her grief and later her amazement (John 19:25–27). Jesus' love is expressed directly and completely to each of us.

But at the same time this love is not idealistic or sentimental. The Pharisees were trying to kill Jesus, and later they did engineer his death. Yet at first they did not fully admit their own motives and twisted desires, or recognize that they were attempting to defend their own empire and dominance. Jesus directly confronted them with the truth – 'You are determined to kill me' (John 8:40) – and gave them the chance to come to terms with what was wrong. This love exposes the wrong to the light, not to gloat or condemn, but so that good can be restored. It does not delight in evil or keep a record of wrongs (1 Corinthians 13:5–6). It does not take wrongs to its own heart to stir up anger, but it is love in truth. It is not to be deceived; it does not take the easy route and pretend that things are fine, but perseveres and hopes in the face of properly identified failure, so that in the end it may rejoice in the truth.

It is not a kind of love which we possess. Our weakness does not allow us to focus on *our* love. In order to be truthful, we must know how deep our failures to love and understand one another really are. Even good and healthy marriages contain appalling levels of ignorance and failure in love. But beneath that failure is God's perseverence and patience with us. As Jesus taught, it is the love which is as close as the child to the breast and also waits through long years for the wayward person to return to an open relationship (Luke 15:11–32). It is God's love on which we depend daily and hourly. It is to be within us as streams of living water. It is, as we ask of God, no longer reactive love, but that which gives and suffers gladly. Those who have it will be given more. It does not dwell on what we deserve, but is marked by undeserved grace. Nobody can crow and say, 'Look at my love,' but each of us accepts whatever love we experience with gratitude to God, humbled. We must receive and be healed.

Yet part of the glory of love is the richness it uncovers. Unloved, we shrivel; but loved, we grow and flower. Many of us rush superficially from one person to another, looking for the best deal. Yet, in the experience of many men and women, those who have been 'rejected' are rich and precious beyond estimation. There are fools who have thrown away the Crown Jewels in their spouse because their lack of love has blinded them. To love is to see and to open up the incredible richness of another person, which is enough to last a lifetime. To love is to garden. God supplies the sun, the rain, the earth and the plants, and we merely tend one another. But who does not flourish under tender treatment?

The central fact is that this love is of God. Jesus gave the love of the Father to the disciples and showed us God's love. Love comes from God to us, and is the truth of our existence to which we respond. We cannot find it except by opening our hearts and lives to God. If we worship or serve any idol of our own creating, it will fill our hearts with limescale and make them brittle for love. Rather, we are to place our lives in the hands of God each day, for God is greater than our hearts and knows everything. This is love: not that we love God, but that he loved us and sent his Son to suffer from and disarm our sin (1 John 4:10). Jesus has gone through the worst failures of love and dealt them the *coup de grâce*. We are led beyond our failure into God's bonus time.

Finally, we remember that this love is also far wider than

the man–woman union which has been our focus here. Now we see how narrow has been the framework of the rest of this book. Because so many of our relationships have become loveless – retailer–customer, banker–customer, employer–worker, driver–pedestrian – we have retreated to the one relationship where we hope at least that love and intimacy will be real. Those who experience loveless family life, especially, seek this elusive love. Everything is invested here. Were love more normal (and this is not to talk down its genuine occurrences), then much of the tension and apprehension surrounding male–female love relationships would dissipate. Thus the wider adventure of Christian love, whereby strangers move into bonds of trust and openness, is the broader response to our specific quest. There is no-one who is not looking for love at different levels, and all of us are capable of giving love in unique and valuable ways which draw on God's love. Many of the answers in the quest for love are not found in a special partner, but in the daily contacts of life and our prayers for them.

But, since it has been the specific concern of this book, let us conclude by focusing on the specific form of love called marriage.

Marital love

Marital love needs to be rooted in God's wider truth and steadfastness, but more specifically it is held within the union which involves a mature man and woman each giving to the other fully – two persons sharing each other for life. This is a union of body, emotions, thinking, relationships, work and money; it shares faith, hopes, failures, sickness, poverty and suffering with joy and reliability, because each partner loves the other – there is no other reason. Sexual union says truthfully, 'I love you,' and the message bears much repetition. In this intimacy, two persons are able to read each other, sharing new pages every day. They practise love on the basis of the security of God's love for them. They learn to be patient and kind, and not to envy, boast, be rude or seek their own happiness first.

They are not self-congratulatory, do not get angry, and do not store up the wrongs and weaknesses of their partners to use later. They enjoy truth which is not degraded by evil; they protect, trust, hope in and persevere for one another. They recognize that love is a command; there is really no other way of living a humane and good life. They trust in God to make obedience to this command a reality in their lives and to see it through until all the other ephemera of life drop away.

Chris hovered in the doorway near the foot of the stairs. Dad was slowly climbing them, leaving his stick hooked over the bottom of the bannister on his way to bed. She was worried about Mum, who was climbing up behind him with one hand supporting his back. The twenty years of Parkinson's disease had slowly taken their toll, and, although Dad's arms were strong, if he fell Mum could do little about it except fall too. She was worried that all this caring was too much for Mum, and came forward out of the doorway, full of anxiety.

It took her a while to take in what was happening. She hadn't heard clearly, but Dad must have said something like 'Your turn now'. Mum moved ahead of him on the staircase, and he put his free hand on her back while pulling up strongly with his other hand until they reached the top and turned into the bedroom. Their love, respect and patience for each other, and their trust in each other, swept over Chris's fear; all their anxieties had been passed on to God in prayer, and she had no right to create problems which had been conquered. She felt hers drain away. When Mum came down a quarter of an hour later to make up the breakfast tray and kiss her goodnight, Chris felt as chirpy as Mum undoubtedly was.

This love is ideal, but not out of reach; one just goes ahead and does it with a kiss, an apology or some work. It is romantic, but only in the sense of realizing repeatedly how wonderful this person is whom God has given one to share for life. It is neither Platonic nor feeling-centred, but involves thinking and empathizing with the beloved, until the feelings are attuned to what is good and ignore the pathetic emotional hiss from other frequencies. This love is dutiful, but not in an impersonal, activity-centred way. Rather, it reaches steadfastly for the partner in whatever situation, and pulls him or her on to good ground. It does what is really needed and carries on loving when there is no reward. In this love there is happiness, but not the kind that is based on a shallow euphoria or an indulgence of our egos. Rather, it is joy which grows out of the truth of the relationship and the astonishing experience of God's overflowing generosity, the sense of a 'good measure, pressed down, shaken together and running over, poured into your lap' (Luke 6:38). Here, there is a sharing of bodies, but not in lust, exploitation or a blind search for sexual experience. By contrast, it is a cherishing, a giving to one another and an affirmation of how good it is to be together. Here, also, there is liking for each other – not the kind that demands a made-to-measure partner who will fit first time, but the kind that comes when the shoes have taken the shape of the feet, and are warm and never felt as something separate. There is also power in this love, but no need for assertion. It always wins, but neither partner does. It attains many things, but always with the haunting awareness of how God patiently interferes in our lives, and how that man, Jesus, always did it first.

How stupid we are to play with counterfeits! The search for love is the same as the search for God, and we find both in Jesus Christ.

BIBLIOGRAPHY

W. F. Albright, *Yahweh and the Gods of Canaan* (Eisenbrauns, 1990).

P. Aries and A. Bejin, *Western Sexuality* (Blackwell, 1985).

D. Atkinson, *To Have and To Hold* (Collins, 1979).

D. Bailey, *The Man–Woman Relation in Christian Thought* (Longmans, 1959).

J. Becher (ed.), *Women, Religion and Sexuality* (WCC, 1990).

G. Becker, *A Treatise on the Family* (Harvard University Press, 1981).

V. Beechey and J. Donald (eds.), *Subjectivity and Social Relations* (Open University Press, 1985).

G. C. Berkouwer, *Man: the Image of God* (Eerdmans, 1962).

G. Bilezikan, *Beyond Sex Roles* (Baker Book House, 1986).

A. Borrowdale, *Distorted Images* (SPCK, 1991).

P. Brown, *The Body and Society: Men, Women and Sexual Renunciation in Early Christianity* (Columbia University Press, 1988).

J. Burckhardt, *The Civilisation of the Renaissance in Italy* (Phaidon, 1965).

D. Clark (ed.), *Marriage, Domestic Life and Social Change* (Routledge and Kegan Paul, 1991).

P. Caplan (ed.), *The Cultural Construction of Sexuality* (Tavistock, 1987).

P. Collins, *Intimacy and the Hunger of the Heart* (Columbia, 1991).

D. Cooper, *The Death of the Family* (Penguin, 1983).

A. Corob, *Working with Depressed Women* (Gower, 1987).

E. J. Dingwall, *The American Woman* (Duckworth, 1956).

J. Dominian, *The Capacity to Love* (Darton Longman and Todd, 1985).

M. Featherstone, *Consumer Culture and Postmodernism* (Sage, 1991).

M. Featherstone, *et al.*, *The Body: Social Process and Cultural Theory* (Sage, 1991).

P. Feldman, *Sex and Sexuality* (Longmans, 1987).

M. M. Fortune, *Sexual Violence: The Unmentionable Sin* (Pilgrim, 1983).

M. Foucault, *The History of Sexuality*, 2 vols. (Penguin, 1981, 1984).

R. Freedman, *Beauty Bound: Why Women Strive for Physical Perfection* (Columbus, 1986).

M. French, *Beyond Power: Women, Men and Morals* (Jonathan Cape, 1985).

S. Freud, *Civilisation, Society and Religion* (Penguin, 1985).

E. Fromm, *The Art of Loving* (Allen and Unwin, 1957).

G. Gaebelein Hull, *Equal to Serve* (Revell, 1987).

P. Gardella, *Innocent Ecstasy* (Oxford University Press, 1985).

R. J. Gelles and C. P. Cornell, *Intimate Violence in Families* (Sage, 1990).

E. Gellner, *The Psychoanalytic Movement, or The Coming of Unreason* (Paladin, 1985).

J. R. Gillis, *For Better for Worse: British Marriages 1600 to Present* (Oxford University Press, 1985).

J. W. von Goethe, *Faust* (1808–32).

A. De Graaf and J. Olthius (eds.), *Towards a Biblical View of Man* (Institute for Christian Studies, Toronto, 1978).

P. Hazard, *European Thought in the Eighteenth Century* (Pelican, 1965).

J. J. Hermsen and A. van Leming (eds.), *Sharing the Difference: Feminist Debates in Holland* (Routledge and Kegan Paul, 1991).

J. Holland, *et al.*, 'Pressured Pleasure: Young Women and the Negotiation of Sexual Boundaries' (*Sociological Review*, Nov. 1992), pp.647–673.

G. Hough, *The Dark Sun: A Critical Study of D. H. Lawrence* (Duckworth, 1990).

A. Jonasdottir, *Love, Power and Political Interests* (University of Orebro, 1991).

E. Kant, *Critique of Practical Reason* (1788: Macmillan, 1993).

H. S. Kaplan, *The New Sex Therapy* (Times, 1974).

S. Kierkegaard, *Works of Love*, trans. H. V. and E. H. Hong (Harper, 1962).

——, *Purity of Heart*, trans. D. Steere (Harper, 1958).

D. H. Lawrence, *Lady Chatterley's Lover* (1928), *The Rainbow* (1915), *Sons and Lovers* (1913), *Women in Love* (1920) (current Penguin editions).

A. Lawson, *Adultery: An Analysis of Love and Betrayal* (Oxford University Press, 1990).

W. E. H. Lecky, *History of European Morals*, 2 vols. (Longmans, Green, 1888).

H. G. Lerner, *The Dance of Intimacy* (Harper and Row, 1989).

C. S. Lewis, *The Allegory of Love* (Oxford University Press, 1958).

——, *Surprised by Joy* (Collins, 1980).

P. K. Lunt and S. M. Livingstone, *Mass Consumption and Personal Identity* (Oxford University Press, 1992).

R. McCloughry, *Men and Masculinity* (Hodder and Stoughton, 1992).

W. McDougall, *An Outline of Psychology* (Methuen, 1928).

J. MacMurray, *Reason and Emotion* (Faber, 1935).

J. A. Mangan and J. Walvin (eds.), *Manliness and Morality* (Manchester University Press, 1987).

A. Metcalf and M. Humphries, *The Sexuality of Men* (Pluto, 1985).

J. Moffatt, *Love in the New Testament* (Hodder and Stoughton, 1929).

D. H. Munro, *A Guide to the British Moralists* (Fontana, 1972).

A. Nygren, *Agape and Eros* (SPCK, 1932).

J. Osborne, *Look Back in Anger* (Faber, 1957).

J. Olthius, *Keeping our Troth* (Harper and Row, 1986).

R. Pearsall, *The Worm in the Bud* (Pelican, 1971).

L. Pincus (ed.), *Marriage: Studies in Emotional Conflict and Growth* (Tavistock, 1960).

O. Piper, *The Biblical View of Sex and Marriage* (Nisbet, 1960).

S. B. Pomeroy, *Goddesses, Whores, Wives and Slaves* (Schocken, 1975).

M. Praz, *The Romantic Agony* (Oxford University Press, 1970).

J. Sarsby, *Romantic Love and Society* (Penguin, 1983).

L. Segal, *Slow Motion: Changing Masculinities, Changing Men* (Virago, 1990).

L. A. Selby-Bigge, *British Moralists* (Bobbs-Merrill, 1964).

D. Spender, *Man-Made Language* (Routledge and Kegan Paul, 1985).

A. Storkey, *A Christian Social Perspective* (IVP, 1979).

E. Storkey, *What's Right with Feminism* (SPCK/*Third Way*, 1985).

——, 'So What's the Difference?' (*Third Way*, Dec. 1987).

L. Tolstoy, *Anna Karenina* (1873–7), trans. A. and L. Mande (Everyman, 1993).

A. Tomlinson (ed.), *Consumption, Identity and Style* (Routledge and Kegan Paul, 1990).

P. Tournier, *Escape from Loneliness* (SCM, 1962).

D. F. Wright (ed.), *Chosen by God: Mary in Evangelical Perspective* (Marshalls, 1989).

T. Walter, *All You Love is Need* (SPCK, 1985).

NOTES

Chapter 1

1 E. J. Dingwall, *The American Woman* (Duckworth, 1956).

Chapter 2

1 S. Freud, *Civilisation, Society and Religion* (Penguin, 1985), pp. 243–340; E. Fromm, *The Art of Loving* (Allen and Unwin, 1957), p. 77.
2 W. McDougall, *An Outline of Psychology* (Methuen, 1928).
3 L. A. Selby-Bigge, *British Moralists* (Bobbs-Merrill, 1964); D. H. Munro, *A Guide to the British Moralists* (Fontana, 1972).
4 D. Spender, *Man-Made Language* (Routledge and Kegan Paul, 1985), pp. 52–162.
5 A. Corob, *Working with Depressed Women* (Gower, 1987), pp. 55–61.
6 W. Shakespeare, *Twelfth Night*, Act I, Scene i.

Chapter 3

1 M. Praz, *The Romantic Agony* (Oxford University Press, 1970).

Chapter 4

1 E. Kant, *Critique of Practical Reason* (1788: Macmillan, 1993).
2 S. Kierkegaard, *Purity of Heart*, trans. D. Steere (Harper, 1958).

Chapter 6

1 H. Mayhew, *London's Underworld*, ed. P. Quennell (Hamlyn, 1950), pp. 31–132.
2 J. Holland *et al.*, 'Pressured Pleasure: Young Women and the Negotiation of Sexual Boundaries' (*Sociological Review*, Nov. 1992), pp. 647–673.
3 H. S. Kaplan, *The New Sex Therapy* (Times, 1974), pp. 523–524.
4 R. Freedman, *Beauty Bound: Why Women Strive for Physical Perfection* (Columbus, 1988).
5 G. Hough, *The Dark Sun: A Critical Study of D. H. Lawrence* (Duckworth, 1990).

Chapter 8

1 G. Becker, *A Treatise on the Family* (Harvard University Press, 1981).
2 T. Walter, *All You Love is Need* (SPCK, 1985), pp. 60–69.
3 P. K. Lunt and S. M. Livingstone, *Mass Consumption and Personal Identity* (Oxford University Press, 1992), p. 90.
4 A. Tomlinson (ed.), *Consumption, Identity and Style* (Routledge and Kegan Paul, 1990), pp. 139–152.

Chapter 9

1 M. Willmott and P. Young, *Family and Kinship in East London* (Penguin, 1962), pp. 1–118.

Chapter 10

1 T. Veblen, *Theory of the Leisure Class* (Kelly, 1991).

Families at the Crossroads

RODNEY CLAPP

'Scant decades ago most Westerners agreed
that lifelong monogamy was ideal . . . mothers
should stay home with children . . . premarital
sex was to be discouraged . . . heterosexuality
was the unquestioned norm . . . popular
culture should not corrupt children. Today not
a single one of these expectations is
uncontroversial.'
So writes Rodney Clapp in assessing the status of
the family in postmodern Western society.

In response many evangelicals have been quick
to defend the so-called traditional family,
assuming that it exemplifies the biblical model.
Clapp challenges that assumption, arguing that
the 'traditional' family is a reflection more of the
nineteenth-century middle-class family than of
any family one can find in Scripture. At the same
time, he recognizes that many modern and
postmodern options are not acceptable to
Christians. Returning to the biblical story afresh
to see what it might say to us in the late
twentieth and early twenty-first centuries, Clapp
articulates a challenge to both sides of a critical
debate.

A book to help us rethink the significance of the
family for the next century.

208 pages   *Large Paperback*

Inter-Varsity Press

Sexual Chaos

TIM STAFFORD

Pornography. Homosexuality. Rape. Date rape. Adultery. Divorce. AIDS. Premarital sex. Sexually transmitted diseases. Teen pregnancies. Single-parent homes. Sexually explicit advertising. Gay rights.

All of these pervade our world as we are rapidly sucked into a vortex of sexual chaos. Not so long ago there was general agreement about what standards should guide sexual conduct. But the old consensus of values has failed to hold the centre in this raging storm.

- How were traditional norms so swiftly overturned by a new, more tolerant ethic?
- Is lifelong marriage still a significant and viable option?
- How can Christians keep from being pulled along by the massive forces of change?
- Is celibacy too little recognized and affirmed in the Christian community?
- What do we make of the debates raging over homosexuality?

These are the questions Tim Stafford responds to with a steady hand and a discerning mind. He clearly explains how and why we now find ourselves in the midst of sexual chaos. But he goes beyond that. In this revised edition of *The Sexual Christian*, he details what a Christian view of sexuality is and needs to be in the turbulent nineties.

This book charts a way to God's ideals for men and women in a society obsessed with sex.

174 pages   *Large Paperback*

Inter-Varsity Press

Gender and Grace
Women and men in a changing world

MARY STEWART VAN LEEUWEN

Sexual identity lies at the core of the crucial questions that we all ask of life. Yet today those questions are ever harder to answer. Traditions about the 'real man' and the 'woman's place' have been challenged. Scientists debate what nature actually dictates for male and female. And theologians engage in heated controversy over what the Bible really says about female submission and male headship.

In this sane yet provocative book, an informed social scientist and committed Christian thinker braves a jungle of confusion to offer unusual insight on the part genes, culture and faith play in making us the men and women we are – and ought to become.

288 pages   *'B' format*

Inter-Varsity Press